# Living in the
# Appalachian Forest

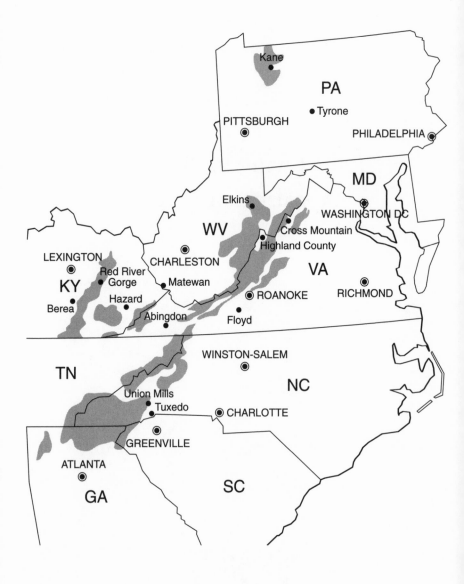

# Living in the Appalachian Forest

## True Tales of Sustainable Forestry

*Chris Bolgiano*

STACKPOLE
BOOKS

Published by
STACKPOLE BOOKS
5067 Ritter Road
Mechanicsburg, PA 17055
www.stackpolebooks.com

Printed in the United States of America

10 9 8 7 6 5 4 3 2 1

First edition

Cover design by Caroline Stover
Cover photographs by Paul Rezendes and the author

**Library of Congress Cataloging-in-Publication Data**

Bolgiano, Chris.
    Living in the Appalachian forest : true tales of sustainable forestry / Chris
Bolgiano.—1st ed.
        p. cm.
    Includes bibliographical references (p. ).
    ISBN 0-8117-2845-5
        1. Forests and forestry—Appalachian Region—Anecdotes. 2. Sustainable
forestry—Appalachian Region—Anecdotes. 3. Forest landowners—Appalachian
Region—Anecdotes. 4. Bolgiano, Chris. I. Title.

SD144.A112 B66 2002
634.8'2'0974—dc21                                                      2002021230

*To the people I met,*
*and the many more I didn't,*
*who are stumbling toward sustainability,*
*this book is gratefully dedicated.*

## Fredrick Verner

My neighbors say, "He is a fool—
Stubborn as his old Jim mule.
A hundred like him could not plow
The land he owns today, and now
He sold his sheep to pay Abe Hall
For that rock heap, and just last fall
He gave O'Kane two hundred bucks
For red oak brush that ain't worth shucks.
He don't half tend to what he's got—
His barns cave in, his apples rot,
The rats eat up his granary store,
But all he wants is land,—and more."

Off to myself, I spit and say,
"Derned if I see it that-a-way,
For sheep may die and good banks bust,
But land's a thing a man can trust."

I've got a hankerin' in my breast,
The kind that gives a man no rest,
To look as far as I can see
And know it all belongs to me.

—From *Gauley Mountain: A History in Verse,* 1939,
by West Virginia poet Louise McNeill

# CONTENTS

# Acknowledgments

ALL THE PEOPLE IN THIS BOOK GAVE GENEROUSLY OF THEIR TIME AND their ideas. My work was also shaped by conversations and correspondence with many others over a period of several years, and if I have left any out of this list, I apologize: Alexander von Elverfeldt, Dylan Jenkins, Maxine Kenny, Steve Brooks, Ted Harris, Jim Minnick, Betsy Taylor, Shireen Parsons, Mark Hollberg, Joe Lehnen, Jim Belcher, Wayne Barfield, Lynne Faltraco, Dee Pardiny, Connie Grenz, Ed Stein, Bonnie Hoover, Frank Adams, David Wheeler, Robert Zahner, Dennis Desmond, Randall White, Ray Elam, Mike Armstrong, Danna Smith, Kathy Newfont, Susan Stout, Caroline Edwards, Than Axtell, Susan Morse, Fred White, Faye Cooper, Rodney Bartgis, Brent Martin, Paul Carlson, Craig Cylke, Dave Maehr, Roy Grimes, Bill Kittrell, Steve Lindeman, Louise Weber, Spencer Phillips, Tom Hammett, Jody Padgham, Jim Birkemeier, and Sandy Schenk. Special thanks go to Susan Lapis of South Wings and to John Cox and Jeff Larkin of the University of Kentucky for aerial photography of clear-cutting and mountaintop removal.

My editor, Mark Allison, made a valiant if unsuccessful effort to find a supplier of certified paper for this book. As always, the staff of Carrier Library at James Madison University has given indispensable assistance. And as always, I am myself sustained by a loving circle of family and friends.

ONE

# OWNING

HOW CAN WE LIVE ON THE EARTH WITHOUT DESTROYING IT? THAT is one of the great questions of our age, ranking right up there with Is God dead? and If so, did the Goddess do it? Actually, all three questions are related. Showing the connections among them, in a manner that relieves plodding philosophical earnestness with mildly amusing anecdotes about real people, is my goal for this book. The people referred to are forest landowners, and their search for sustainability is what this book is about.

"Sustainable" is the buzzword of the millennium. It appears globally, prefixed not just to forestry, but to every other aspect of human occupation of the planet: agriculture, fisheries, communities, cities, landscapes, tourism, business, nuclear waste management, mining, landfills, development. Wait a minute. Sustainable landfills? Sustainable development? Aren't these contradictions in terms? Are we going to hear next about sustainable overpopulation?

The problem is that the concept of sustainability is so new to industrial society and so revolutionary in its ultimate, all-encompassing meaning that it defies definition and remains vague enough to keep everyone happy. Sustainability for some multinational corporations, for example, means always having another country to colonize. Sustainability to a developer might mean always having another rare species to name the new gated community after. Sustainability to the average American seems to mean always having another mall to shop in.

Well, you get the point: As we define sustainability, so goes the world. Because the world depends on forests to provide such niceties as clean air and water, forestry practices have become a primary target for exercising the meaning of sustainability. It's high time. Nearly half the world's land was covered with forests ten thousand years ago, as human societies began to organize around agriculture. Since then, at least a quarter of the world's forests have been demolished, most of the remainder suffer from exploitation and pollution, and even they are disappearing as forestland is converted to other uses, such as crop fields or parking lots.

Loss and degradation of forests are not good for the global environment. Climate change, leading to floods, droughts, and species extinctions, which in turn lead to the disappearance of sources of food and other necessities for human survival, is intimately linked to forest health. The United Nations tried to address these concerns at the 1992 Conference on Environment and Development (called the Earth Summit) in Rio de Janeiro, Brazil. It proposed a set of agreements known as Agenda 21, promoting international action against deforestation, but this failed to become a formal treaty. Instead, it contributed to the rise of a conspiracy theory about an imminent U.N. world takeover, involving black helicopters flying nocturnally over remote rural areas of the United States. So far, there is only anecdotal evidence to confirm this belief.

Besides paranoia, there is another impediment to changing the way forests are treated, and it is, of course, money. Trade in forest products accounts for about 3 percent of the global economy, but much more in the individual economies of particular developed and developing countries. The single most striking fact of global wood use is its importance as fuel. The majority of the world's people are so poor that they rely on the nearest forest to cook their meager meals and warm their shivering bodies in winter. Slightly more than half of all wood cut around the world every year is burned as domestic firewood. In some developing countries, fuel is the final use of nearly every tree cut.

That still leaves an annual woodpile of more than a billion and a half cubic meters harvested for industrial purposes—about five hundred Great Pyramids of Khufu, each of which covers thirteen acres. This wood is sawn into lumber, pulped for paper, and manufactured into plywood and other panels, in that order of importance. Global demand for all these products nearly tripled during the second half of the twentieth century, thanks in large part to Americans. With a third of its landmass covered by forests, the United States has historically been a wood-oriented nation. Today it takes a dual lead as the world's largest producer and consumer of industrial wood, generating about a quarter of the world's entire output but consuming closer to a third. Because the average American uses five times as much wood as the average Third World resident, the United States is the world's leading importer of forest products, mostly pulp and paper from Canada. At the same time, it is second only to Canada as an exporter of wood products, largely pulp and paper. Stand on any major highway across the continent, and chances are good that you'll see similar loads of logs being hauled in opposite directions. The inefficiencies of the market are inscrutable.

The wood market is divided into two basic categories: softwoods, which you can indent with your fingernail, and hardwoods, which you can't. Softwoods constitute well over half of the world's industrial harvest and are used for construction lumber and paper. They generally come from coniferous trees, which are evergreen with needles or scalelike leaves. Pines, spruces, firs, larches, hemlocks, cedars, redwoods, sequoias, and a dozen other conifers grow in the temperate zones, the two climate belts between the tropics and the polar circles, but most notably in the Northern Hemisphere.

The tallest and stoutest conifers in the world grow in the ancient forests of the Pacific Northwest in North America. Because of the relatively mild climate, abundant moisture, and long-lived nature of the trees, some trees grow ever larger for a thousand years or more. So attractive are these huge trees for timber that by the 1980s the original forests had been virtually eliminated on private lands in the United States, and cutting was moving rapidly onto public lands owned by various agencies of the federal government.

It's a quirk of industrial civilization that as people earn their livings in ways no longer connected viscerally to the natural world, they reevaluate their environment. To those with leisure and money to spend on enjoying it, the natural world appears in a different light. Instead of a place where physical sustenance is hunted or harvested, forests become scenic settings offering psychological comfort. In a world dominated by science and technology, forests offer a place to feel closer to something sacred. Affluence allows people to put a value on wooded landscapes in a different coin than dollars' worth of timber. Personal economies become influenced by heart and spirit as well as by money.

The towering forests of the Pacific Northwest had that effect on a lot of people. Many felt that the last remaining virgin stands on public lands should be preserved. The resulting controversy was imbued with religious fervor, as those who believed that forests were created for human consumption clashed in court and in the woods with those who felt that old growth was a cathedral rather than a crop. Arguments centered on a small, shy bird known as the spotted owl, whose numbers may or may not have dropped as the forests disappeared—no one is really sure how many there were or are. Even so, the unconventional view that non-human beings have value in their own right, whether or not they are useful to people, successfully challenged the status quo. Nearly twelve million acres of softwoods on public lands were removed from timber production to protect the owl. Appeals of one kind or another are likely to go on for years.

But even the spotted owl controversy pales beside the international furor over tropical hardwoods. Roughly a third of the world's harvest of industrial wood is composed of hardwoods. Hardwoods in the temperate zone are mostly broad-leaved deciduous species, the kinds of trees that lose their leaves and sprout new ones every year in seasonal rhythms; in the tropics, many hardwoods are evergreen.

Harder and stronger than softwoods, hardwoods are used in a wide variety of solid wood and plywood products, as well as in paper.

Until recently, much of the world's hardwood harvest came from tropical rainforests. Due to widespread publicity, rainforests are now famous for their astonishing biodiversity and the remarkable rate at which it is being lost. Half of all known plant and animal species live in tropical rainforests. During the 1980s, an area of rainforest larger than the state of Georgia disappeared from the world every year, a pace that accelerated in the 1990s.

As images of rainforest destruction circulated the world, Europeans, especially Germans, who have perhaps the most sophisticated environmental consciousness in the world, began to reject products made from tropical hardwoods. Producing countries naturally resisted being told what to do by nations that had already cut all their own virgin forests. Inevitably, supplies of tropical hardwoods began to dwindle as forests were exhausted. At the same time, possibly in response, but more likely just because of the caprice of fashion, world taste shifted toward lighter shades of wood than those of dark tropical hardwoods. All of these factors coalesced to open a market window—more like a set of double doors, it turns out—for hardwoods from temperate zones.

And as it happens, the world's greatest concentration of temperate hardwoods grows in the eastern United States. Cherry, ash, poplar, oaks, maples, and two or three dozen more species that grow across the East have long been globally popular for their light color, as well as many other attractive qualities. Indeed, the rich, textured gleam of furniture made from fine American hardwoods is an international status symbol. So sought after have they become that income from exports of eastern American hardwoods multiplied by 500 percent in less than a decade, to reach some $2 billion a year by the end of the twentieth century. The eastern United States now supplies nearly half of the world demand for temperate hardwoods. This explosive rate of export growth is not considered sustainable by industry analysts, who know a financially cyclical business when they audit one. Nonetheless, all trends point toward continuing demand for American hardwoods, because as developing countries develop, they emulate our own excessive consumption habits.

American hardwoods reach their fullest potential in that state of mind and country called Appalachia. Roughly defined as the southern half of the Appalachian Mountains, here is manifested a divine delight in biodiversity. More than two thousand species of plants, and still uncounted numbers of animal life forms, form the most diverse temperate forest in the world. What this means on the ground is a quiet green riot of woodlands. Nuances of life bewilder the senses and frustrate the taxonomist. New species are still being discovered regularly. The relationships among this abundance of living forms are Gothic in their vaulting architecture. Maybe that's why the Scots-Irish settlers, with their Gothic mindset of the Celtic kind, invested the Appalachians with ghosts and fairies.

But that happened very recently in a place where life's time line stretches very far back indeed. These are the forests that time has chosen for its own. Afternoon light, dripping like honey from green leaves, the curve of a turk's-cap lily, the fragrance of a fringe tree, all pass in momentary splendor. Yet here, beyond the reach of scouring glaciers, above the pounding of seas, have passed some two hundred million years of steady plant evolution. Here began the development of trees from club mosses and horsetails into palm-like cycads, then magnolias and ginkgoes, then conifers, and finally the flowering hardwoods. It was a piece of luck to end up here, and I intend to belabor you with my appreciation of it.

When my husband and I bought a hundred wooded acres in the Virginia mountains twenty years ago, all I knew was that the forest looked beautiful to me. On matters of its history, its health, and its harvestability, I was blissfully ignorant. In this I was representative of my type—that is, the category of people that professional foresters call nonindustrial private forest owners (NIPFs). Unlike the western United States, where most forests are owned by the federal government, in the East, less than 10 percent of all forested landscapes are federally owned. Southern Appalachian forests are distinguished by a unique core of public lands, but even so, most mountain forestland is held by several million private hands. The number of private ownerships increases every year as forested real estate is fragmented into ever smaller tracts. It is the greatest experiment in private forest ownership in the history of the world.

Like the forest itself, American private forest landowners are so diverse in motives and agendas that foresters have despaired at ever understanding them. "What do NIPFs want?" is the perennial question of professional forestry. There's no simple answer, because NIPFs include people whose ancestors homesteaded the land, outsiders who migrated from the cities, descendants of those outsiders, owners of small tracts and huge estates, absentee owners, nonprofits and profits, institutions and organizations of every kind. Many of these landowners are united by nothing more than legal title to adjoining properties. Some have long ties to particular places. In Appalachia, NIPFs may own more forestland than industrial owners, but it's the coal and timber barons that have more profoundly impacted landscape and people. Much as they'd like to be left out, industrial owners can't be excluded from any discussion of sustainable forestry.

The real people who populate this book are Appalachian forest owners who reflect all that diversity, but they aren't representative. On the contrary, I've sought them out because they are pioneers, exploring what sustainability means in a postindustrial forest. Whether from motives of purity or profit, all are exploring a new path, a middle route between preservation and exploitation. It's a serpentine trail across slippery slopes in every direction. The only reference point is the forest itself. The changing, changeable woods are the textbook from which instruction must be taken. Lessons may not be what you expect.

I have learned to watch for the occasional day on Cross Mountain when nature shows her most murderous face. It happens only every few years. The last flare of autumn in fallen leaves is first extinguished by sodden winter. Then temperature and moisture may conspire with evil intent. The dark hump of mountain through my western window turns deathly pale in a fine mist. Raindrops gather at the ends of bare twigs, to freeze into blades of ice. Ice dulls the green of the cedars to the color of doom. Sometimes the air is still and suffocating. Sometimes there are gusts of wind like tracer bullets across the forest floor, tossing up helpless leaves. If I ventured out unprepared, Cross Mountain would kill me with hypothermia in a few hours. On such days, I feel most deeply my love for this place.

Although I lack personal experience with motherhood, I suspect this feeling is akin to the love of a mother for her serial killer child. It is an unconditional, unreasoning, undeniable love. Its power takes me by surprise. I am disarmed, but I am not, after all, rendered so witless that I want to go outside today. Instead, with the requisite cup of homegrown herb tea, I sit at the window, savoring the ironies of emotion and environment by watching to the west.

For two decades, Cross Mountain has filled my western horizon. It rises at the edge of the Shoemaker River valley, west of the much wider Shenandoah Valley. Staring out at it, but unable to see more than a few square yards, I sit with arms hooked over the back of a chair at the window, alert for any activity in the gloomy light outside. Small creatures have fled, seeking cover in cedar trees and under brush piles, but two deer come to lap up spilled corn from the squirrel feeder. They stand quietly with heads down. It's snowing, and the white flakes on their dusky backs turn them once again into spotted fawns. With binoculars, I look them over possessively, gauging their robustness. How much fat on their ribs? How bright their eyes? I think of them as my deer, because they live mostly, perhaps entirely, on my hundred acres. Of course, I know they belong to no one but themselves. It's just that I've been corrupted by ownership.

When I was young, all I dreamed of was land. If you've never experienced a phenomenon called land hunger, I can only tell you that, like an addiction, it can command every aspect of your life. I caught it from my husband, a biologist and woodsman. Together, we spent more than a decade driving on real estate forays, looking for land in the mountains. Passing the lovely old farms that line the narrow valleys to the west of Cross Mountain, I would ache with longing to belong there. Owning acreage was our entire agenda. I wanted to live in the privacy of my own property, not answerable to any person in sight. To eat from my own garden. To be warmed by my own firewood as I sit in front of my window, watching winter.

The deer have disappeared. Snow is collecting in the gashes made by old logging roads, soft like the buzzard down that Indians used to stuff into wounds. Like the pioneers that drove out the Indians, I am not native here. Like them, I left family history behind in Europe. Genealogy has always seemed to me to be a pointless pursuit. My ancestors were either handsome or plain, smart or stupid, kind or cruel. Or, if they were like most people who ever lived, they were all of these at various stages of their lives.

I have no ancestors buried on Cross Mountain, their bones to become part of the trees and the deer. Neither have I descendants for whom to lay up an empire. How then, without these two primeval human ties to place, to explain my attachment? Peasant genes from the Old Country, no doubt—my great-grandmother was a miller's daughter. Or maybe it's the simple fact of being an exile. Unable to feel at home on any continent, maybe I was vulnerable, a sucker for wherever I settled down. I chose Appalachia and have been trying to cope with the consequences ever since.

Heritage is a game of truth and consequences. Fully a product of Western genes and capitalist culture, I am a control freak and frankly proprietary toward my real estate. Ownership is righteous. It is engorged with the power of the state. Our borders are well marked, although at the moment, in this mist, I can't see beyond any of them. Wait—the fog drifts away momentarily, and I recognize Reedy Ridge. In that instant, I realize how acutely conscious I am of borders. Not having grown up here, I know this place by its boundaries rather than by its extent. It is not yet for me a landscape of life events. On the other hand, there is a value to being an outsider without a vested interest in defending the past.

Within my own borders, I may do pretty much as I wish, and what I wish is to protect. That is the benefit of owning: to protect what you love. At its best, possessiveness is composed of equal parts righteousness and a sense of safekeeping. There's a lot of talk about private property rights but much less about private property responsibilities. What do I owe the many communities of Cross Mountain for the privilege of living within them?

Cross Mountain doesn't get its name from its shape, because it forms a U, with a ridgeline hovering around a modest elevation of twenty-one hundred feet. Inside the U, somewhere in the heart of the drainage, I once found what appeared to me as the most beautiful creek in the world: bedrock stepping down in gray slate ledges, each filled with limpid pools in which many large fish swam. I've never found it since. Sometimes I wonder if it was magic, but Cross Mountain is not known for magic of any sort. Aside from the obvious fact that it has a name, Cross Mountain is quite anonymous. All the reports I read when we first bought land here—soil productivity assessments, wildlife habitat ratings, dependability of stream flows— ranked it fair to poor. No special areas were identified. The foresters we consulted all agreed that the trees were typical mixed Appalachian hardwoods. We should not expect anything beyond the ordinary on Cross Mountain.

Yet I have found such uncommon plants as fringe trees, round-leaved orchis, lily-leaved twayblade, and red mulberry trees. A blinking saw-whet owl one autumn afternoon earned me a county bird club first sighting record. Warblers rare for this area, like Wilson's and orange-crowned, flit through. Ravens nest along the top of the mountain, and woodcocks have danced near its foot. Wood turtles appear occasionally, apparently expanding the southernmost extremity of their range. In addition to all the predictable varieties of small wildlife, I have found salamanders and snakes of mysterious species (at least to me). I have seen a mink, a bear, and a bobcat. Cross Mountain is a classic example of revelation, through time and conscious attendance, of hidden depths below the surface of understanding.

The surface of the ground outside is becoming glazed now, as the snow turns to sleet. If this keeps up all night, even the lowliest ground dwellers will have trouble finding their next meal. On such days as these, when Cross Mountain unleashes its deadliest powers, I recall to mind as an invocation its opposite mood, the bluebird days of spring, when skies are mild and dogwood blossoms spangle white across the unfurling green of the forest. On those days I sit out on my deck to soak in the blessings of air and light, and to mind the mountain. I listen for the songs of migrating birds and watch the slopes and hollows that course down Cross Mountain to see what's going on, which is usually nothing obvious. It was on one of those days in our early years here that I first heard someone hot-rodding out on the dirt road, undoubtedly throwing beer cans as he went. The roar broke the forest stillness and voiced everything I feared in life, defiled everything I held sacred. My anger leapt until I cursed the driver with a vehemence that, afterward, astonished me. I found myself flushed with hatred. I understood then where all the anger in the world comes from, the intensity that lights wars. It comes from me.

There are other lessons I'm learning from Cross Mountain. The cedar in front of the deck obstructs the panoramic view from my window, but once, after a deep snow had buried the forest floor for weeks, I saw bluebirds, robins, and cedar waxwings, famished, search out the tree's blue-black berries. Having glimpsed the role of that single tree, I begin to sense the whole in the part, the universe in the atom. I see that the forest is like human society. Each tree is an individual, wounded by life in idiosyncratic ways, yet inextricably a part of something larger than itself. When a tree dies, it molders calmly to show how easy it is to return to earth, in the process that nurtures us all.

With the forest as example, I can fit myself into the inexorable cycle of life and death. It's the only way I *can* fit in. Without ancestry or progeny here, I have no past in this land, and no future. I have only the present moment, the eternal present of forest life. Just at this moment a branch in the cedar tree is shedding its icy load in a cascade of razor-edged shards. I'm glad to be sitting here with steaming mug in hand, safe inside, where there is mint instead of murder in the air.

# THE LANDLESS

A DIFFERENT KIND OF MURDER WAS ON MY MIND AS I WOUND through the mountains of southern West Virginia. Mountains rose against the horizon like a choppy ocean, a series of steep, stationary swells interrupted by odd levels of flat plains not formed by any natural process. I turned off Route 97 onto Route 52 toward Justice, a few miles north of Panther. Between those two names lies a whole world of stories about people and place. And the graveyard of America's favorite feud.

This is Hatfield and McCoy country. Or, more accurately, Hatfield country. The McCoys lived—and still do—thirty miles to the southwest, across the Tug Fork River, which forms the border with Kentucky. The Hatfields lived—and still do—right here in Wyoming County and in the neighboring counties of Mingo, Logan, and McDowell. You see their names on mailboxes along the roads. The name that you see even more often, though, is Lester.

I followed the Guyandotte River past a hollow where founding father William Lester once owned a large tract of land. He traveled here from western North Carolina in 1808 to homestead the land granted him for service under George Washington in the Revolutionary War. There wasn't enough money in the young country's treasury to pay him in cash. William brought his Cherokee wife and three children, one of whom, a little girl named Dorcas after her mother, drowned while crossing the New River. Seven generations later, William Lester's great-great-great-great-grandson Todd welcomed me into his rented home. Where William once farmed and hunted on his own wide holdings, Todd has only the hope of inheriting thirty acres of his grandmother's old farm. In that shrink-wrapped history is packaged all that has gone wrong in Appalachia, all the shining promises that turned to dust—black and smeary from the coal mines, fine and parching from the torn forest floor.

It's only right to start a book about owning land in Appalachia with an account of landlessness, because that is the region's essential paradox. The log cabin and the split-rail fence, the long rifle hanging on a buckskin-clad shoulder, the quilts that pieced frugality into art—these are beloved images of American self-identity. And not just the image but the reality, in woods-wise and independent settlers like William Lester and his family. Under almost unimaginable hardship, they perfected a set of skills for living a good life in the great Appalachian forest. These men and women were the sturdy yeopeople in Thomas Jefferson's (gender updated) vision of democracy.

But William Lester was in the minority. Relatively few of the families that homesteaded the mountains were ever able to purchase enough land to support themselves. Much of Appalachia was owned from the start by distant speculators and a small number of affluent local elites. Tenancy and sharecropping became as typical for mountain people as sovereignty on their own farms. Many of those who did own land had it stolen from them during the half-century holocaust of coal and timber extraction throughout the region that began in the 1880s.

In the 1980s, a coalition of volunteers called Appalachian Alliance produced a seven-volume survey of rural landownership across eighty counties and twenty million acres, mostly in the coal-bearing areas of the mountains from West Virginia to Alabama. They found that 40 percent of the land and 70 percent of the mineral rights were held by corporations, mostly coal but also timber. Three-quarters of the land was owned by absentees. Poor people in the mountains stayed that way in large part because they neither owned the land nor shared in the wealth it produced. In the two decades following the survey, regional poverty rates declined by nearly half, due largely to federal monies and an unprecedented surge of grassroots community activism. Still, parts of Appalachia, particularly some of the coal counties, continue to rank among the most poverty-stricken in the nation. And yet, despite the alienating forces that have rendered him landless, or maybe in some way because of them, Todd Lester has the most holistic vision possible of a sustainable forest: one with cougars in it.

Todd is a third-generation coal miner in his midthirties. A slight, wiry man with dark hair and eyes, he is soft-spoken and retiring in the way of many mountain people. He grew up hunting and roaming the woods. The year before he graduated from high school, one evening at dusk when he was out hunting raccoons with his dogs, Todd saw something he'd never seen before. A large cat with a long tail was stepping stealthily down a slope, saw him, then turned and raced back uphill. It was a cougar.

Called panther or catamount by many early settlers, and mountain lion or puma by later pioneers in the West, the cougar was the top predator in eastern forests when Europeans arrived. The cats' soundless, solitary stalking was better adapted to deep woods than the chasing habits of wolves. Their need for fresh meat was more demanding than the wolf's acceptance of carrion or the black bear's omnivorous rummagings. Many mountain stories tell of cougars dropping from trees onto unsuspecting people, or covering a sleeping person with leaves as they do to cache their prey, or screaming like a woman being murdered. Cougars were feared for their undetectable presence and their ambush attacks, and rightly so: A 1751 gravestone in Pennsylvania marks the earliest recorded human death due to a cougar, although undoubtedly not the first, and most definitely not the last. In the West today, cougar attacks are a serious consideration when hiking, or at least they should be, because attacks occur almost every year, although fatalities are extremely rare.

With wolves and bears, cougars form a natural triumvirate of predator power. Early settlers found it impossible to live with any of the three large mammals. People generally viewed nature as an enemy to be conquered. Wilderness and wild creatures had value only insofar as they could be transformed into goods and services that served human ends. Predators in particular embodied the worst aspects of nature, the bloody death of innocents. Even worse, predators, especially cougars, meant competition for the same game animal—deer—that provided rural people with one of their most valuable forest products. By the late 1800s, wolves were extirpated from the East, and bears almost so. Bears recovered somewhat after public lands were established to protect habitat and hunting was regulated. Whether any native cougars survived has become a world-class wildlife mystery, like Nessie in Scotland and the Yeti of Nepal.

Sparse and scattered in the early twentieth century, cougar sightings by the last quarter of it had swelled to such a volume that they became a phenomenon in themselves. Thousands of people have reported a glimpse of rippling cat muscle and long, low-slung tail. Some found the experience powerful enough that it charged their view of the world with a new kind of emotional, if not spiritual, energy. Of all those I've met during twenty years on the eastern cougar beat, Todd is the most convincing.

"When we made eye contact," he said, "the cat captured a piece of my heart."

Cougar sightings are notoriously inaccurate. Western biologists have found time and again that coyotes or bobcats are commonly reported as cougars. Sightings are therefore rejected as evidence by the official wildlife establishment—state and federal wildlife agency administrators, field biologists, and academic scientists. Throughout the twentieth century, these officials consistently denied the possibility that wild cougars could exist in the East. Sightings were attributed to drunkenness, delusion, or deception. When Todd tried to talk to the West Virginia wildlife authorities, they rudely dismissed him. He remained quietly certain of what he had seen and gradually became determined to prove it.

After he graduated from high school, Todd heeded his parents' advice to avoid the mines and joined the Air Force. Stationed in Florida, he met Frank Weed, a famous breeder of cougars for the pet trade and a self-proclaimed expert on the Florida panther. Todd spent hours studying Weed's caged cats, and more hours in the hardwood hammocks and the flat piney woods studying panther sign in the wild. After four years, he came home and, because there was little else, went into the mines.

In his free time, he began to search for cougars in West Virginia and surrounding states. He posted flyers in country stores asking people to call him if they saw a cougar. Calls came in slowly at first but grew steadily in volume. Todd developed a system for logging the calls, and those that sounded most convincing sent him out to the woods. Between calls and field trips, he married Jaquetta, whom he calls Quett, and had a daughter, Shanda, who inherited his soft, brown eyes. Sometimes they go out in the woods with him. Quett sends out ads for Todd's cougar hotline to seventeen free weekly trader newspapers. She often takes incoming calls, although as a miner's wife her heart chills when the phone rings late at night during Todd's shift. After she graduated from the local community college with a degree in computers, Quett taught Todd the basics. He quickly established an Internet website and a listserv on eastern cougars, which attracted members as distant as Brazil. Cyberspace is where I met him. He would make a little joke and then type, "SMILE."

As he continued his fieldwork in the real world, his pretty brick house with Quett's pots of petunias hanging on the porch became an archive. One room was filled with shelves of three-ring binders organized by topic and stuffed with articles, studies, reports, and letters. File cabinets crowded around the desk and computer. Large plastic storage tubs held reports of sightings. A seven-state map covered one window, with dots for last year's sightings. Walls were covered with cougar pictures. There were photos of tracks and deer kills, boxes full of plaster casts of tracks, some videos, and a couple of hair samples. It was a painstakingly assembled body of evidence that just might document cougar presence.

In 1996, it did. Todd e-mailed scanned photos of plaster casts he made of tracks at a nearby creek to a cougar expert in California whom he met on the Internet. By systematically calculating angles between toes and pad, the biologist declared the tracks to be definitely cougar. An expert from the Florida panther project also looked at a photo of Todd's track casts and confirmed them as cougar. The place where Todd found the tracks was not far from where he saw the cat in 1983. Through all those years, Todd consistently recorded evidence of cougars in that area, including females with kittens. It was one of several historic places Todd took me when I visited.

Todd drove a red pickup truck with fancy license plates that said "COUGAR," a gift from Quett. Roads here mostly follow the many creek bottoms of this well-watered land, where tributary after tributary spills into the gathering Guyandotte. Every time we switchbacked up a steep mountainside to cross over a ridge, a coal truck was ahead of us, laboring and spewing soot. From the top, we got quick glimpses of expansive views before we zigzagged down again. Most of the houses were crowded along the narrow valleys. Few, if any, human habitations perched on the mountain slopes or tops.

It was summer, and the forest-covered mountains were green and fragrant. Sourwood trees were in bloom, flinging out spiky fingers of little white bells like dancers. Bees danced around them. Once, sourwood honey stolen from the bees was part of the seasonal round of life here. The forest was a harvest ground, and its rich biological wealth supported a correspondingly varied human economy. Knowledge of the forest and how to use it for food, medicine, shelter, and tools constituted a distinct Appalachian culture. Not that mountain life was any "harmony with nature" idyll. Many of the old farm and forest practices were destructive. But any chance for improvement, any possibility for realizing the sustainability inherent in the skills and the small-scale impacts of traditional Appalachian life, was overwhelmed by industrial-scale resource extraction.

It started with timber. Many families had been impoverished by the Civil War. When shortly afterward agents of timber entrepreneurs from the outside world began to filter into the mountains, buying land outright or rights to it, they were welcomed. Cash was the scarcest commodity around. Men walked many miles for dollar-a-day jobs on the logging crews. Foremen, log scalers, and wagon drivers earned even more. Along with the jobs came rising demand for farm products, which in turn stimulated the establishment of stores and trading centers. In only a few decades, logging transformed an intensely agrarian and largely self-sufficient society into an industrial, wage-based one, causing no end of social turbulence. So it's not surprising that timber was the root cause of the Hatfield-McCoy feud, not ancient animosities, or unrequited love, or, as big-city reporters told it, simple backwoods barbarity.

The Hatfield family cemetery lies across Island Creek a few miles northwest of Todd's house and is approached by a decaying 1932 bridge restricted to foot traffic. At the entrance is an arching iron sign that says "Hatfield." Nearby is a plaque stating that the cemetery was placed on the National Register of Historical Places in 1995. Catbirds complained as we walked up the rough, stony road. Two cedars reared dark and imposing like sentinels along the way. One bore a sign:

Posted
Protected by Law
Wildlife Sanctuary
Registered with the Brooks Bird Club, Inc.
An international organization.
Headquarters Wheeling, WV

Graves marked by plain fieldstones with initials scratched into them dotted the slope. A recent grave showed raw, red dirt. Far more people are buried here than were killed in the feud, which ended in 1890 after a dozen years with a total of a dozen dead. Stones continued back into a thick, young forest that rose up the slope. There were plots for little babies and aged elders. Even people buried fifty years ago had bright, new silk flowers on their graves. The oldest part of the cemetery was probably the half dozen rocks whose scratchings were no longer legible. The earliest birthdate discernible was 1866. One stone had "Sarah A." chiseled on it, probably the Sarah Ann that the nearest town was named after.

The agave plants that mark old homesites had multiplied around the forest edge, and some had tall flower stalks. Daisies and other wildflowers spotted the shaggy lawn. A singing wood thrush competed with the rumble of coal trucks down on the road. There were several obelisks, a lamb, and a cross, but what dominated the cemetery was a life-size marble statue of Devil Anse Hatfield, enclosed by a black iron fence. He stands straight and sturdy in jacket and breeches with a long beard curling down his chest. In 1921, at eighty-one years old, having since the age of thirty-nine been one of the two major principals in the feud, he died in his bed.

Devil Anse, born William Anderson Hatfield, was a guerrilla leader for the Confederacy during the Civil War and widely respected as an expert horseman and marksman. His nickname derived from a single-handed fight with a cougar in his youth, after which his mother declared that he wasn't afraid of the Devil himself. Devil Anse was energetic and ambitious, but his prospects after the Civil War were dim. Large families and the practice of dividing up land among the children had used up the small amount of tillable acreage in the tightly confined valley bottoms, and there was little capital to venture into anything else. But Devil Anse was not one to work as a hired hand for neighbors, as many of his contemporaries had to do.

In 1869, he established his own timber company in partnership with a brother-in-law. He hired a logging crew and marketed timber from the lands of relatives. He quickly gained a reputation for being an imposing adversary, dogged in pursuit of business interests, but honest. In the 1870s, he filed a lawsuit against a young neighbor named Perry Cline for timber trespass—a complaint that was becoming increasingly common—and won Cline's five thousand acres. Cline moved across the Tug Fork to Kentucky.

Timbering soon became the Hatfield family's primary business, involving most of Devil Anse's brothers and sons, as well as others who had no family connection. They felled huge oaks, ashes, walnuts, cherries, and white and yellow pines, but especially poplar trees, some of them six feet and more across at the stump. Oxen teams hauled the logs to the banks of streams. Crews branded the logs, chained and pinned them into rafts, and floated them down to local merchants, who then moved and marketed the timber farther downstream in Catlettsburg and Cincinnati. Devil Anse became wealthy. Entrepreneurship was not a valued trait in that traditionalist agricultural society, and his success did not sit well with some people.

Randolph McCoy was older than Devil Anse and, like him, well known, but for different reasons. His father, Daniel, had stolen timber from another man's land and lost his farm to pay back the debt. After fifty years of marriage, Daniel's wife divorced him because she was sick and tired of the brutal way he treated her. Their son Randolph, known as Old Ranel, showed similar traits and was generally regarded as a crank. Old Ranel's business endeavors, including timbering, did not fare well.

The earliest record of what was to become Old Ranel's obsessive rancor toward Devil Anse appears in 1878, when he filed a complaint against a Hatfield cousin for stealing a pig. The offense was serious; a pig was an important economic investment and could mean the difference between hunger and fatmeat. There must have already been something divisive between the families, because the judge carefully appointed a jury of half Hatfields and half McCoys. The Hatfield was acquitted when a McCoy relative testified in his favor. Clearly, values other than clan loyalty were operating, because there were Hatfields and McCoys who sided with each other, Hatfields and McCoys who stayed completely neutral, and several dozen supporters in each camp that weren't kin at all.

Family alliances became further entangled when Roseanna McCoy, dark-haired daughter of Old Ranel, fell in love with Johnse, the handsome, flirtatious son of Devil Anse, and moved into the Hatfield household, where she was welcomed. This was not unusual. Mountain women had some degree of sexual freedom, and illegitimate children were generally accepted without discrimination. After six months, though, a pregnant Roseanna returned to her family, possibly because of Johnse's continuing dalliances with other women. Shortly afterward, Johnse married a different McCoy. There seem to be no recorded objections from either family.

A year later, Devil Anse's brother Ellison was stabbed and shot, apparently without provocation, by three of Old Ranel's sons. Ellison was carried to a house near Mate Creek on the West Virginia side of Tug Fork. The local sheriff had apprehended the three McCoys and was taking them to jail across the Tug Fork in their home county in Kentucky when they were captured by Devil Anse and a posse of twenty. Devil Anse held the McCoys until word came that Ellison had died of his wounds. He then blindfolded and tied the three young men to trees, asked for their last words, and executed them.

"You push a Hatfield," said the plump, middle-aged lady at the Hatfield Information Center, "and they'll push back." Her husband, now deceased, was Devil Anse's grandson. The center was located just down the road from the cemetery in a trailer with lawn statues in front and a sign that read, "Hatfield Flea Market, Used Work Clothes." Mrs. Hatfield sat at a desk piled with magazines and newspapers, and the surrounding space was jammed with shelves of books, videos, and tapes, all concerning the feud. The walls of the cramped hallway were covered with photographs.

"My husband's dream," said Mrs. Hatfield, "was to show people what his grandpa was like, a good man but pushed too far."

Devil Anse's retaliation for his brother's murder was extreme in a law-abiding society where murder was rare. Yet it offered a rough form of justice. Officials in Pike County, Kentucky, indicted Devil Anse and his posse, but despite Old Ranel's shrill demands, for five years no one was interested in serving the warrants or requesting extradition of any Hatfields from West Virginia. Here the feud surely would have ended, unnoticed by the world. But during that five years, the Norfolk and Western Railway began surveying for a route through the region. The coming of the railroad meant that timbering, which had been relatively small-scale because of limited transportation, could expand spectacularly. Coal mines could also be developed. And it looked like the railroad might go right through Devil Anse's land.

By this time, Devil Anse's former neighbor, Perry Cline, who years earlier had lost five thousand acres to Devil Anse's lawsuit, had become an influential politician in Kentucky, aligned with the outside capitalists who sought to develop timber and coal. He was also a distant relative of Old Ranel McCoy. Cline saw his chance, and in 1887 he persuaded the governor of Kentucky to enforce the warrants outstanding against Devil Anse and offer rewards for the capture of all relevant Hatfields.

What had been a feud between families erupted into a war between states. Bounty hunters pursued Hatfields through the woods. A Kentucky posse led by a notoriously unsavory character invaded West Virginia and captured some Hatfields. A West Virginia posse, not including Devil Anse, who often tried to avoid violence, burned Old Ranel's home and killed two McCoys. Old Ranel escaped by hiding in the pigpen. A pitched battle was fought between the two posses, with one man killed. The shooting ended when nine Hatfields and their associates were tried in Kentucky, and one, called slow by some and dim-witted by others, was hung for murder in 1890. The press had a field day.

With the paradoxical twist native to Appalachian history, Devil Anse, who began as a challenger to the old mountain culture, ended as one of its proudest symbols. He became a grand old man even as his earlier influence waned. Investors from outside the region drowned him and other small, local operators in a flood of capital and a political system designed to channel it away from local pockets. Devil Anse lost dozens of court cases as competition for timber intensified. Creditors forced him to pay off his debts by selling his land for half its value to a group of Philadelphia coal speculators. Two years later, as railroad tracks were laid, it was worth ten times as much. Devil Anse was defeated but not reduced to penury. He bought a piece of mountain land near Sarah Ann and retreated into a barricaded compound to live out his days hunting and making whiskey as mountaineers always had. Estimates of the number of people at his funeral in 1921 range from five hundred to five thousand. Old Ranel died unnoticed a few years before Devil Anse, still railing bitterly against him.

The feud ended not with a bang, but with the rasp of saws. Whole mountainsides were denuded as industrial forces triumphed. Most trees of any value were cut, removing the seed sources of desirable species. Trees were wrenched out in careless and destructive ways, and the limbs and branches left behind fueled unnaturally hot wildfires that burned the soil. Soil eroded quickly and deeply. Deer, wild turkeys, bears, even rabbits and squirrels became scarce in many places. The last remaining predators died out or retreated to the most remote and inaccessible crags. West Virginia had been almost completely forested at the start of the twentieth century but was almost completely denuded by 1920, and what happened there mirrored what was happening elsewhere across the mountains. When the timber was gone, a few people were rich, but many others had become dependent on a false economy, without even the forest to fall back on for meat and fuel.

The deforestation of Appalachia was one of history's great examples of unsustainable forestry. The resulting floods and siltation of navigable rivers prompted Congress to pass the Weeks Act of 1911, authorizing the federal purchase of private lands in mountainous headwater areas. Taxpayers footed the bill for U.S. Forest Service and National Park Service efforts to end the wildfires and reestablish forest cover. By the 1960s, more than seven million acres of national forests and parks along the highest spine of the southern Appalachians had taken their current shape of two Rorschach blobs connected by strings. They constitute the largest complex of public lands east of the Mississippi River. It is this unique backbone of public land, and the opportunities it offers, that distinguishes Appalachia from other eastern bioregions.

But no public lands were purchased in coal country, where private companies had obtained title or rights to most acreage. Companies used deceit and even murder of unwilling sellers to get land. Nearly fourteen million tons of coal were coming out of McDowell County annually by 1912, and coal operators were busy setting up company towns like feudal estates in the surrounding counties. African-American laborers from the Deep South and immigrants from Eastern Europe were brought in under conditions of peonage, a practice started by the timber companies. As for local men, the desperate need for another source of wages after the timber was gone rendered even the fiercest Hatfields and McCoys vulnerable to terms offered by the mines.

Like dispossessed peoples everywhere, mountaineers had three choices. They could escape by uprooting themselves from family and homeland and moving elsewhere in search of livelihoods. Migration to factory cities across the Midwest became a fact of Appalachian life throughout the twentieth century. They could rebel through personal lifestyles that rejected the Victorian middle-class propriety being imposed upon them. Poverty has aided and abetted those mountaineers who delight in flaunting class differences, especially in the delicate matter of trash in their yards. Last, and most compellingly, they could adapt. Devil Anse's brother Elias was a particularly successful example. After the feud, he moved to the county seat and prospered as a councilman, constable, chief of police, and private detective. One of his sons became governor of West Virginia, and his granddaughter married the president of the U.S. Steel Corporation.

U.S. Steel owned the land that Todd and I drove through after we left the Hatfield Cemetery. Occasionally we'd see one of their signs at a mine opening, an inconspicuous if heavily concreted entrance on a hillside. Every once in a while we passed an enormous, elaborate house. It stood out in the neighborhood like . . . well, like a mansion among mobile homes.

"Coal operators," Todd said. "It's easy to tell."

We were heading toward Matewan, a small town on the Tug Fork, where a sort of sequel to the feud took place, far less known although it also involved a Hatfield. Born in 1893 on the Kentucky side of the Tug Fork, Sid Hatfield was not directly related to Devil Anse and may have been illegitimate or even adopted. Nonetheless, he grew up to display Hatfield characteristics of energy and ambition. After he finished school, he moved across the river to the bustling new town of Matewan and went into the mines. Like other miners, he had to sign the obligatory "yaller dog" contract forbidding him to "affiliate with or assist or give aid to any labor organization." Like other miners, he saw friends maimed or killed by accidents and black lung.

Matewan was almost exactly as old as Sid, having been founded when the Norfolk and Western Railroad reached the bend on the Tug Fork where Mate Creek comes in. An early homesteader named the creek in memory of his favorite hound dog, Mate, who had chased a black bear across the frozen mouth of the creek sometime in the mid-1800s. The weight of the animals broke the ice and both drowned. The town of eight hundred wasn't originally named after the creek, but for Matteawan, New York, home of one of the railroad engineers. Local residents quickly changed the spelling and pronunciation.

The odd name was highlighted as the title of a 1987 movie made by John Sayles about the Matewan Massacre. Sayles had heard about the 1920 shoot-out when he hitchhiked through the area and talked with old folks. It wasn't until after the movie came out, though, that people began to speak openly about what had happened, and about the rest of what has come to be called the mine wars. Battles raged off and on for decades as miners tried to unionize.

"There's no statute of limitations on murder," said the lady behind the desk at the Matewan Visitors Center. "And some people blew up bridges so trains couldn't move. It was taboo to talk about it." Nor was it covered in most history books or school curricula. Todd's grandmother, for example, who was born shortly after the Matewan Massacre and only a few miles away, first learned about it as a young adult when she happened to read an article in *True Detective* magazine. The pattern of withholding facts continues: Todd had never heard of acid rain, a critical forest problem caused by burning coal, until I mentioned it to him.

The Matewan Visitors Center is housed in the Hatfield Building, erected in 1911 by a son of Elias Hatfield between the railroad tracks and the Tug Fork. Wood and masonry structures line the block. In 1920, there was a jewelry store owned by the mayor, a department store, and a restaurant run by a coal company informant who conveniently provided a meeting place for the United Mine Workers of America. There was a hotel used as headquarters by a gang of detectives from the Baldwin-Felts agency, a firm based in Bluefield, West Virginia, that supplied men for hire by the coal companies as armed guards, strikebreakers, and spies. There were hardware stores, general stores, drugstores, saloons, gambling dens, and houses of ill repute. And a depot. Along the tracks at the depot is where it happened. Bullet holes still scar the wall of the Matewan National Bank.

Sid Hatfield played pool and poker and slot machines. He drank and smoked. Although small and slender, he earned the reputation of a highly competent fighter. With his high cheekbones and jaunty air, he was often chased back by the women he chased. He became a friend of Matewan's mayor, who appointed Sid as the town's first chief of police. Unlike most other elected or appointed officials in the region, neither of them was in the pay of the coal companies. When miners got drunk or rowdy, Sid took them home or looked the other way. Twice he was himself arrested for fighting and making moonshine, but Sid was so popular that both times the mayor posted his bond and put him back on the job.

Early in 1920, the bushy-browed president of the United Mine Workers of America, John L. Lewis, launched an organizing campaign in southern Appalachia. The union had succeeded elsewhere in getting better conditions and more pay, and southern Appalachian miners knew it. Sid stood watch evenings at the Matewan Baptist Church as miners met to learn about the union. When famous labor advocate

Mother Jones arrived to make her rousing speech about "medieval West Virginia," Sid escorted her. Miners lost their jobs by the hundreds as they joined the union, and some mines were forced to close.

The Baldwin-Felts men, locally known as thugs, evicted the fired miners and their families from company-owned homes, tossing entire households onto the street. The union somewhere found land to rent and opened tent colonies for the homeless. Reporters wired back stories about barefoot children in the snow.

In May, thirteen thugs arrived in Matewan on the noon train. They climbed into waiting automobiles and drove to a mining camp, where they turned six families out into the rain. When they returned to the depot to catch the five o'clock train back, Sid and a group of miners stopped them. As they argued over warrants and jurisdiction, the first shot boomed. Instantly, a barrage followed. The detectives ran, and one swam across the Tug Fork, but seven fell dead. Two miners and the mayor also died.

It's said that people in Matewan still argue about who fired that first shot. Sid opened himself to charges of a hidden agenda when, two weeks after the incident, he married the mayor's widow (with several of the mayor's approving relatives in attendance). Sid and twenty-two others were tried for murder, but no local jury would convict any of them. Over the next year, tensions flared ever higher as tent colonists skirmished with state police, striking miners shot at working miners, saboteurs dynamited coal equipment, and martial law was declared. Fifteen months after the Matewan Massacre, Sid and a colleague were summoned to the McDowell County seat of Welch to stand trial for blowing up a coal tipple. They were given safe passage by the governor. Climbing up the stone steps of the courthouse, unarmed, with their wives beside them, the two men were assassinated by thugs.

The Matewan Visitors Center displays a union badge worn at the funeral. Two thousand people walked in procession across the swinging wire footbridge over the Tug Fork to a cemetery in Kentucky. In the following weeks, as word spread, miners streamed down mountain roads and filled up trains, black men and white men, native born and immigrants, carrying guns and talking of avenging Sid's death, until they coalesced into an army of ten thousand men marching toward Matewan. Many wore the blue bib overalls and red bandanas that had come to signal union men. They were called "rednecks." They commandeered vehicles and trains. For a week, they controlled five hundred square miles of southern West Virginia. It was the largest insurrection since the Civil War.

On Blair Mountain, they met with several thousand state police and volunteer deputies, who generally thought of the miners as drunken louts that were perpetuating personal feuds. The casualty rate was amazingly low, due to rough terrain and an absurdly ineffective early use of aerial bombs. Sixteen people were estimated killed, although the exact number will never be known. But when the U.S. Army was called in, the miners stopped shooting. Many of them had served in World War I just three years earlier and still wore their old uniforms. They were too patriotic to fight Uncle Sam. Some miners surrendered; most just slipped away home.

Blair Mountain was not the last battle. In fact, with coal providing half of the electricity generated in this country, the mine wars are still going on. As we drove away from Matewan, Todd pointed out a mine where a guard was shot during a strike in 1986. Unions did finally become established in the 1930s, under President Franklin Roosevelt and his pro-union wife, Eleanor, and conditions for miners improved substantially. But unions have been losing ground lately. The mine companies are now such huge, mechanized conglomerates that they can hold out against a strike in a way the older ones couldn't. In addition, some coal companies are keeping the union out by paying higher wages than union mines.

Todd works in such a mine, a fact that pains his father. "I've always been a strong union man," Jackie Lester said, when we stopped by to visit. A small, neat man, Jackie and his wife, Sharon, live in a double-wide on four and a half acres. "These four counties, especially, have been for the union, but nonunion has now taken hold. It used to be you could work all your life for one company and retire from them, but not now." Jackie was able to retire because his quarter-century membership in the union had secured him a pension.

He had learned about mining from his father, who began working punch mines in the 1950s. These were holes punched into a hillside leased from a coal company, along with all equipment. Five to ten miners drilled and blasted for coal, then loaded it by hand into a metal car on rubber wheels pulled by ponies.

"You could make a good living," Jackie said. "It was hard but honorable work." As a ten-year-old, he would go in the mine during the summer, not to work but to watch, maybe run errands. "It was a way of life. I worked at the sawmill for $1.25 a day for a while, but the mines paid better," he remembered. His brother also went into the mines, only to be pinned by a coal car that broke his spine. "We walked him twice a day in a cast to get him mobile again," Jackie said. He and Todd joked about all old miners having lost a few fingers. Just like old loggers.

Over the past decade, Todd worked for three or four different companies in eight different mines and had no pension other than a Keogh plan. Currently he worked the midnight to 8 A.M. shift, sometimes six days a week. More than once he had been on his way out the door to work when the phone rang and he was laid off until further notice. He hadn't bought a house out of fear of being saddled with a mortgage and no work. He'd been hurt several times, including a broken arm, but did not report all the injuries because he was afraid they would jeopardize his chances for jobs at other mines.

One payday Todd went to the office as usual to find several of the big bosses standing around in suits and ties. As the miners queued up for their checks, the bosses asked them to sign petitions in favor of a mining practice called mountaintop removal. Just as its name implies, it removes the top of a mountain through blasting and pushes the rubble into the nearest valleys. Its amazing scale of destruction has prompted lawsuits and other, more emotional challenges from a wide range of people. Todd felt trapped, sure to be fired if he refused. "So I scrawled my name so nobody could ever read it," he said.

Mountaintop removal is the latest in coal extraction techniques. The method that preceded it was called strip mining, to which Jackie graduated after spending five years in the deep mines. Stripping meant longer hours but more pay, and it was much safer, being above ground. You can see strip mines across many of the mountains, contour lines of bare, vertical cliffs with compacted ground at their base, making the hillsides look terraced. "Strip mining could have been a lot better if they'd just restored it right," Jackie said. "They should have been required to plant apple trees and hardwoods for wildlife. And the state never enforced the surface mine regulations the way they should have."

Jackie also thought logging was underregulated and did a lot of damage as well. Recently he had lost sixteen trees to timber poachers. "What I regret most is the way the bulldozer tore the land up," he said. His own father had spent two years in the Civilian Conservation Corps, an environmental jobs program created by President Roosevelt during the Great Depression of the 1930s. The young men of the corps helped stop erosion after the turn-of-the-century timbering, fought wildfires, and planted trees. Temperate climate, abundant moisture, and a diversity of tree species able to take advantage of a wide range of conditions gave Appalachian forests a remarkable resilience. But the forest that grew back was hardly the same. Second-growth trees will never get as big as virgin growth, because damage to soil will limit productivity for centuries, if not millennia.

Nonetheless, a functioning forest reappeared, with its own distinct characteristics. By the 1930s, wildlife was returning with help from deer, turkeys, and fish stocked by state game departments. In places where the virgin timber had been harvested before 1900, by the 1930s the second growth was beginning to support a sawmill industry again. It was a heartening measure of how far regeneration had advanced to hear from Jackie that trees were once again valuable enough to poach.

It became clear when we drove through the tiny town of Justice that the rising timber values of recent years had not gone unnoticed.

To my great disappointment, Justice was named after a man, not a principle, but capitalized on the pun with the motto "a right fair little town." There were two sawmills with large lumberyards and a string of big houses along the creek. These belonged to the local Harless family, which had become rich through both timber and coal. They were known for their generous contributions to a handsome new community center, as well as to state and national politicians who favored their interests.

We passed the new community center on the way to the place where Todd had found cougar tracks in 1996. Todd turned off from the main route along the Guyandotte River onto a narrow, paved road up one of its tributaries. The road turned to gravel, then dirt. We passed a few houses, a white clapboard church with "1873" painted above the door, and a lonely satellite dish left behind when a trailer was moved. Then nothing. As we curved endlessly around one hollow after another, I glimpsed strip mines and flattened, grassy mountaintops. Occasionally Todd, who is a deep miner, would point somewhere and say, "We've mined all under that ridge." But it was hard to visualize the dark maze of tunnels beneath an overwhelming impression of green forest, thousands of square miles of it. Not only was it great cougar habitat, but more to the immediate point, it was open to us for the searching. We needed no permissions from property owners to travel through it, because most coal company lands are not posted. Except at mine entrances, fan areas, and power stations, there were no No Trespassing signs. Nothing more than the appropriate state licenses are required for anyone to hunt, fish, trap, dig ginseng and other herbs, or pick mushrooms, ramps, and berries. The very companies that so dramatically changed the physical landscape have—so far—preserved the human psychological landscape of the commons.


Read any historical treatment of southern Appalachia, and you'll come across the use of mountain slopes and ridges as a commons, especially at higher elevations. Few families could afford to purchase the extensive grazing lands required to maintain livestock. So they fenced in their cultivated fields, which were mostly down in the creek bottoms, and let their hogs and cattle run loose on the nearest slopes. The pigs thrived on chestnuts and acorns, and the cattle grazed on the grass that came up after farmers periodically burned the forest. Men hunted game wherever it roamed, and women and children foraged for seasonal edibles wherever they grew.

This pattern of land use applied not just in Appalachia, but in rural landscapes around the world. The idea of the commons is age-old and long predates any notions of private property. Even today, about two-thirds of the world's forests are publicly owned. The commons has been a topic of lively international debate since Garrett Hardin's 1968 paper in *Science,* titled "The Tragedy of the Commons." The gist of Hardin's argument was that individuals who use commonly held land will inevitably exploit it to the detriment of the community, and furthermore, that human population growth is the root cause.

Thirty years later, Hardin's theory holds only too true for what we now acknowledge as the global commons—the atmosphere and the air we breathe, the oceans and the fresh water we drink, and the biological diversity that supports all life cycles. Today the air carries toxins into even the most pristine reaches of the North and South Poles, fisheries are crashing all around the world, and life forms are being extinguished at an unprecedented rate.

After Hardin's paper, international policy wonks decided that privatization was the answer to Third World "backwardness," which was defined as the practice of holding land in common, usually by tribal or traditional peoples. Privatization became one of the World Bank's criteria for awarding development loans. But it didn't take too many years before researchers in the field saw that disaster often followed. It turns out that Hardin's theory is only partially right. The tragedy of the commons applies where no one entity takes responsibility for what happens to the common property, and no accepted mechanism exists for making and enforcing community-based land use decisions. Where such mechanisms do exist, and there are examples around the world, commons have been utilized sustainably for many human generations.

Coal country, however, is a compromised commons. How much so soon became apparent.

Todd drove slowly and peered out the window for tracks along the side of the road. Tracking in the Southeast is much more difficult than in the West, because road dirt here lacks sand and tends to bake too hard in the sun to carry an imprint, and winter snow rarely lasts longer than a few days. Todd is always alert for other kinds of evidence. He stopped suddenly for a large scat in the middle of the road and whipped out the rule from his belt: almost one and a half inches wide, with hair and bones, in three pieces, tapered at one end but not twisted like those of canid species tend to be.

"Could be cougar, but could also be coyote," Todd said. He reached for his supply of plastic bags and prodded the item into one with a twig. There were labs that could test it. Black-throated green warblers were trilling and buzzing above us. Once or twice when we stopped at other places, I heard the fluty song of a wood thrush. Over the course of the day, we found coyote tracks and bobcat and fox scats. There were fresh deer droppings just about everywhere. In places where we walked off the road into the woods, the drop in temperature from the hot, muggy day was amazing. Along the creeks, the understory was deep green and ferny, with rhododendrons in full bloom and lots of mossy logs to trip over.

"This is what I like best," Todd said. "Just being out in the woods." He pointed out raccoon tracks in the mud at a beaver pond. He used to hunt raccoons and won many competitions, and for years he bred a well-regarded line of coonhounds. It was tempting to use hounds to search for cougars, as was common practice out West, but Todd didn't want to harass the cats. After all, they were an endangered species.

Eastern cougars are listed on the federal Endangered Species List, but officials have found a way to sidestep that fact. They can no longer deny the physical proof: In addition to Todd's track, verified field evidence in more than a dozen incidents from Maine to Missouri has confirmed the existence of at least a few cougars living wild in areas where they've long been absent. So much persuasive evidence has accumulated that the wildlife establishment is beginning to acknowledge it, sort of. Officials are routinely quoted as saying that, yes, there may be a few cougars out there, but they're all escaped or released captives from elsewhere, not the eastern cougar subspecies at all. By implication, these cougars aren't entitled to federal protection. It's a handy way to avoid responsibility for a wide-ranging and sometimes threatening predator.

And officials are undoubtedly right in claiming that some cougars are former captives. There's an astounding market, legal and illegal, in large felines. Endearingly cute as kittens, cougars grow into voracious, unpredictable adults. Inevitably, some have been released or have escaped, and there are several known cases of declawed pets surviving many months on their own, even climbing trees. News stories about a cougar sighted in some city or other pop up regularly across the country. Then, too, there are occasional rumors that hunters have brought some into the East to chase, or that radical environmentalists have released some.

"Regardless of their bloodlines, wild cougars deserve to be protected," Todd said as he maneuvered the truck up the last stretch of rough road to the site of the 1996 track. "Nobody can tell eastern and western cougars apart in the woods. Now there's even a DNA study that shows very little genetic variation among all subspecies of cougars. A cougar from anywhere could fill the eastern cougar niche. But I hope against all odds that a majority of the cougars in the East are descendants of native cougars. This is definitely good cougar habitat now, and old-timers say there were always deer and bear and turkey in some parts of this country. I think there have always been cougars, too."

Todd had grown so tired of having his views dismissed for lack of credentials by state wildlife biologists that he started an eight-month course in wildlife and forestry through the International Correspondence School. He was behind, though, he admitted, and needed to get some work turned in. I knew he'd been busy setting up an organization called the Eastern Cougar Foundation, because he had asked me to be vice president. He wanted to do whatever he could to help cougars survive. "I'm not really sure why I'm so drawn to the cougar," he said. "I had never really even thought much about cougars till that moment when I saw one. But one thing is for sure—it changed my life in a real big way."

Through his love and knowledge of the forest commons, Todd sensed the wholeness that cougars confer. No ecosystem can be biologically (or, some say, spiritually) complete without its top carnivores. Cougars embody and exert the evolutionary forces (or, as some put it, the wisdom) of eons. In the grandest sense, sustainability means allowing these forces the scope to continue playing out. In this way, cougars are a critical measure of a sustainable ecosystem.

Large carnivores usually need the largest home ranges of all wildlife, so protecting enough forest for them ensures that many other creatures with lesser needs will also thrive. In the southern Appalachians, a cougar needs somewhere between 25 and 125 square miles of personal space, depending on terrain and the abundance of deer. Accommodating the four to five thousand cats necessary to sustain a long-term regional population will therefore require large expanses of forests connected with one another across many landscapes and ownerships. And at the center of cougar habitat, there should be a core refuge of wilderness where cougar interests are acknowledged as paramount. In this way, cougars demand the ultimate in human humility.

We climbed out of the truck at the place where Todd had found the track. It had been only four years ago, but then he'd had to walk all day to get in. Today the new road was still raw from the bulldozer. We had just driven past a huge fan blowing funky dead air out of a mine and could still hear it. The place where Todd had seen a cougar in 1983 was just on the other side of the knob, so we continued on. A new road led to it, too, with a fan and a sediment pond at the end. Power lines followed the road. "It doesn't look anything like it did when I saw the cat," Todd said. "The road we're on was a deer trail then."

The mines were expanding, both below and above ground, but that wasn't the only reason for the new roads. As the mines reached toward the final seams, there was talk of a post-coal economy. Recreation was an obvious choice for investment. A coalition of community, state, and federal agencies formed in the early 1990s to tap the recreational potential of coal company lands through development of a Hatfield and McCoy Trail System. Aimed at off-road vehicles, it will run for over two thousand miles along the mountain ridges of seven West Virginia counties. In 1994, the state legislature amended liability laws to give landowners (read: coal companies) protection from lawsuits, and in 1996, it established the Hatfield-McCoy Regional Recreation Authority. Upon completion, the trail system is projected to bring in six hundred thousand visitors and $107 million annually and create thirty-two hundred new jobs.

"I'm already finding less and less sign of cougars since these roads started going in," Todd said. He figured there were maybe five to ten cougars at most in southern West Virginia and southwest Virginia. "There's likely to be more up north in the Cranberry Wilderness, but there's about a hundred miles and some interstate highways that cougars would have to cross between here and there."

The Cranberry Wilderness is a thirty-six-thousand-acre permanently protected roadless area in the Monongahela National Forest. It's one of nearly fifty congressionally designated wilderness areas in the southern Appalachian national forests. In these public lands lies the possibility of a bioregional core refuge for cougars. Inherent in them also is the potential for a more dependable commons than private land can offer. Yet even the promise of the public lands as a core of commons isn't enough for cougars. Only if those public lands are embedded in supportive landscapes of private ownership will cougars be able to travel in search of unrelated mates.

With plenty of cover and plenty of prey, cougars are limited only by human tolerance. It seems possible that cougars could, on their own, establish reproducing populations, if people were willing to tolerate them. Cougars offer us a second chance, an opportunity for true sustainability. But using the forest in ways that allow cougars to survive, and by extension all other native life forms, will require a collective social desire to do so. Sustainability is, first and foremost, a state of mind.

My own state of mind was somber as Todd drove down out of the mountains to the Guyandotte valley. History has been harsh here. At the convenience stores and sub shops where we stopped to buy soda, people's faces were gaunt, drawn, hard. Sometimes it seems to me that Appalachia's past can bequeath nothing but darkness to the future. Then I met Todd's grandmother. Hattie Stacy is a friendly, smiling, lively woman with short, curly hair lightly streaked with gray. From the ceiling of her living room hung a quilting frame. She had made more than 160 quilts with friends or by herself and brought some out to show me—bright, beautiful ones with wedding ring or dogwood or poinsettia patterns. Growing or making almost everything was a way of life, and she remembered buying only sugar, salt, coffee, and flour. It was her part of the family farm at Muzzle Creek that Todd would inherit.

As a child, Hattie would run onto the front porch to see a car, so uncommon were they. Her father ran a store but went out of business during the Depression, when he let people have food on credit. His great-grandmother and a child had been captured by Indians and rescued from a tent by a scout, who held his hand over the baby's mouth. Hattie's grandfather was a famous outlaw. "He killed seven men and was probably murdered in turn," she said. "He was shot in the hip by a bounty hunter and went to the pen. But he soaked his shoes in turpentine till the dogs couldn't get his scent, then he broke out. He hid out in the woods and snuck home to get food." She shook her head. "There was always a few mean ones around," she said, neatly summing up a legendary dimension of Appalachian culture.

"In my day," she continued, "bear, deer, skunks, and foxes, both red and gray, were very abundant. So was ginseng, and we would go out senging. My grandma went senging one time and a cougar followed her out, she saw it jumping over logs as it was coming alongside her." When I asked her what she thought about Todd's work, she said, "I think it's great. I'm glad he's doing it. I'd like to see cougars and other animals come back. I'd like to know they're there. We used to have wolves, too. Our kids have lost so much."

Most of the men Hattie knew had gone into the mines, and as I headed toward home, I decided to see what mining life had been like. I stopped at the Exhibition Mine in Beckley, West Virginia, "the city with a mine of its own." The company town was represented by buildings moved from a coal camp near the New River during the first half of the twentieth century. The superintendent's house was a three-story Victorian. The miner's house was a three-room cottage.

The mine itself was older than the model town, having been worked from 1890 to about 1910 by the Phillips family. The seam was thirty-six inches thick at two hundred feet below ground. Visitors ride through some of the nearly seven miles of underground passages on a sort of open streetcar guided by a veteran miner. As we entered the tunnel, there was a blast of cool air and the sound of water running. Drops plopped on my head. The height was just enough for ponies to walk; the men lay on their sides or stomachs to work. The stables were in the mine, and the animals went blind from lack of light.

The tour included several stops at which our guide, who had spent twenty-one years as a miner, pointed out particular features relevant to mining history. He demonstrated how men used augers and tampers in the early days to blast and pick. He described how the men had to purchase or lease all equipment from the company, how they worked ten or more hours a day and earned 20 cents for a one-ton carload. After a 1920 law prohibited child labor, a miner had to be eighteen. The first miners' lights burned coal oil, lard, or cottonseed oil. Thousands died in explosions when the open flames ignited methane and coal dust. There was little, if any, compensation paid to the widows and children. After the guide had explained how the check tag on a coal car would sometimes be switched so the miner couldn't get credit for it, the fellow next to me raised his hand and asked, "Didn't the miners get mad about being taken advantage of?"

"I'm not supposed to get into that; it's a touchy subject," the guide replied.

The restroom was equipped with electric hand dryers. Women and children pressed the button and shook their hands a few times, then hurried off, impatient, leaving the dryer to blow hot breath from the lungs of ten thousand miners into the empty air.

# Just How Beautiful Is Small?

Mounds of broken limbs loomed out of a dense fog. Mist blurred the twisted entanglements of severed roots and stumps. Mud splattered on my boots from a road gouged by heavy equipment. I tripped over pieces of shattered bedrock. A shroud of fog blocked out everything but this trampled battlefield of a war the trees had obviously lost. With muddy piles of debris giving the mist a sepia tint, it could have been a photograph from a century ago, a reprise of the past as if we've learned nothing from a painful history of loss. It was a picture of pure ugliness.

Pretend you are a buzzard (not pretty, maybe, but vastly underrated for flying ability). You lift off from the torn end of a tree limb thrust out from a pile of slash. The billow of mist burns off below as you rise into the sun. You spiral higher and higher above Doe Mountain, and more and more of Giles County, Virginia, spreads out beneath you. As the landscape widens, the clear-cut becomes a small blotch in the midst of several thousand acres of mostly unbroken forest. This is the picture that Britt Boucher, a forester on the cutting edge of sustainability, had in mind when he designed the clear-cut.

"There are actually two clear-cuts here," he said. "Each one is relatively small, about thirty, thirty-five acres. This was an old pasture that had been taken over by mixed hardwoods that were badly broken up by ice storms and a hurricane a few years ago. There was very little financial value in the trees, and it wasn't for the money that the owners decided on a clear-cut. In fact, we had to put these two cuts with a selection harvest of nice red oaks on a lower slope in order to get any loggers to do it. Even then we only sold the clear-cuts because the buyer's wood procurement forester was young and inexperienced."

Between the two cuts, a strip of forest that followed the course of a small spring was left untouched. "It should serve as a corridor for deer to travel into and out of the clear-cuts," Britt said. "There's not much browse for deer on the higher elevations of Doe Mountain. Most of the forest is composed of mature trees that grew up after the mountain was logged around 1900. So for the next thirty years or so, until the new trees start to get taller than the deer can reach, all the stump sprouts that will come up in the clear-cut should feed a lot of deer. The landowners like to see deer around, and some of them hunt."

Britt's youthful face—blue eyes and fair skin surrounded by curly blond hair—belied a maturity of vision. A forestry entrepreneur, he and a partner had started their own business shortly after graduating from the School of Forestry at Virginia State Polytechnic Institute in Blacksburg. Every year across the United States, more than two thousand forestry students graduate with bachelor's or master's degrees or Ph.D.s. There are three major lines of work open to them: wood products industries, state and federal land management agencies, and independent businesses that provide forestry services to private landowners.

Consulting foresters, as these last are called, consider themselves the only entity that can truly represent the interests of nonindustrial private landowners without influence from industry or politics. Clearly, they are an idealistic group. Their professional organization, the Association of Consulting Foresters, was founded in 1948 by a handful of people and has grown to over six hundred members. They are committed to a code of ethics that demands loyalty to clients, service to society, and an approach to business in which advertising is done "only in a dignified manner."

The website for Britt's business, Foresters, Inc., was impeccably sober and so discreet that I could find only one of the mascots for which his software is named. The story of Two Dog software involves not just a beloved pair of pets, but also a significant encounter with an eponymous Indian when Britt was traveling years ago in the Southwest. The software applies high tech to a function that foresters call, somewhat adolescently, cruising. Foresters cruise a woodlot to estimate the board feet of various grades of lumber. A board foot is one inch thick by twelve inches long and wide. It's a common measure in the United States, but most of the rest of the world uses cubic meters to measure volume (one board foot equals .00348 cubic meters). A log can be measured by three different scaling systems: Doyle, International, or Scribner. Its potential lumber is graded according to fine nuances of valuation based on tree species, health, and appearance. The math gets complicated quickly, so a laptop in the woods with the right software makes it much easier to calculate an accurate timber inventory.

Britt now had fourteen employees, although it was touch and go some months to make payroll. Roughly half of his staff worked on computer development. The other half worked out in the field, performing the more traditional task of consulting foresters, which is to plan and supervise timber sales. Britt infused the management plans his staff prepared for clients with findings from ecological research. He supported Todd Lester's Eastern Cougar Foundation in its advocacy of cougars. He was committed to working toward certification from Smartwood, an expensive and controversial process. The Smartwood brand name designates wood products guaranteed to come from ecologically harvested forests, giving consumers the option of supporting sustainable forestry by buying certified wood.

Even at home, on three acres in a rural residential development, Britt tried to build networks of contiguous landowners to make an ecosystem perspective possible. He felt that if the goal was ecosystem sustainability, then the method must be ecosystem management. "But foresters have been talking about ecosystem management for at least a decade without really being able to put it into practice," he said. "To gain any kind of ecosystem control means getting different landowners together, usually many different landowners. It's getting even harder as forests are sold in smaller and smaller parcels. The landowners all have to cooperate, and then there has to be cooperation within the forestry infrastructure. That's just not part of the culture. The culture of forestry is competitive. Loggers rip off the landowners and sawmills rip off the loggers. Big industry drives it all.

"Getting customers who are adjacent isn't random, because word of mouth between neighbors can work for you," he continued. "And I did target Doe Mountain. Still, it's unusual to get three large contiguous landowners as clients. I try to pool knowledge and let everyone know what everyone else is doing. The tract with the clear-cuts is the smallest, and it's a thousand acres." It even had a name: Knipland.

Knipland is a limited liability corporation, a form of business partnership, composed of fifteen family members. The founding parents, who purchased the land in the 1960s, were a famous entomologist named Edward Knipling and his wife, Phoebe. "Knip," as he was known, helped develop chemical pesticides in the 1940s. DDT was credited with saving many lives in World War II by preventing the spread of typhus to American and Allied troops, and for his work on it, Knip received a medal from President Truman in 1947 and the King's Medal for Service from Great Britain in 1948.

Knip had grown up on a farm in eastern Texas and knew what suffering the cotton boll weevil and livestock screwworm fly could inflict. But the farm had also instilled in him a lifelong passion for nature. Early on, he saw the hazards of pesticides and searched for more benign methods of control. His greatest success was the sterile insect technique, in which a target pest species is mass produced in the lab, irradiated for sterility, then released into the environment to mate with wild, fertile insects without producing progeny. Populations of the pest usually plummet. The technique was adopted by governments around the world. In the 1990s, Knip received national and international honors, including an award from the Food and Agriculture Organization of the United Nations. He died in 2000.

"We want to perpetuate my father's vision of conservation and sustainable use," Knip's son Edward said when I called him at home in Maryland. He belongs to an ownership category found across Appalachia: multigenerational absentees. "My siblings and I wrote the bylaws of our organization to limit ownership to family members and to nurture the ethic of sustainability. We operate like a business, with capital gains and so on, but we put all the receipts back into the property. There's no distribution of money to owners. We never intend to sell or make a profit. There's five of us on the board, myself and siblings, the older generation. Part of our estate management is to give our children shares; they're mostly young professionals now, maturing, with families of their own. We'll bring them gradually into the organization.

"The decision to clear-cut was not made casually," Ed continued. "It was a culmination of five years' work. It was methodical and orderly, although we couldn't get the loggers to clean up the last couple of loads. It just wasn't economical for them. One thing we did insist on was protection against erosion. As far as aesthetics is concerned, the worst is right after it's done, like you saw it last summer." I hadn't even mentioned the gloom-and-doom fog. "Since then we've had a bulldozer spread the debris mounds over the ground to rot. The skid trails and landings were smoothed and seeded with a mix of native plants for wildlife. Next spring, there will be some grasses and wildflowers. There already were some wildflowers this fall. In four or five years, it will take on a healed appearance, with new trees coming up."

Ed had hired Britt after one of the family members, a mechanic, worked on Britt's car and got to talking to him. Because of his connections with other landowners on Doe Mountain, Britt knew that the two clear-cuts on Knipland were likely to be the only forest openings on the upper mountain for quite a ways and for quite some time. In that nexus of space and time lies the secret of sustainability.

Since the dawn of human consciousness, people have found an element of the sacred in these dimensions. Sacred time was marked by rituals that often focused on transitions, like prayers at dawn and dusk, and ceremonies at equinoxes and solstices. Rituals today mark transitions in human life, such as christenings, weddings, and funerals. Sacred places once were everywhere. Today, in our society, they are generally limited to churches, cemeteries, and battlefields.

Space and time appear to be the two fundamental dimensions by which we perceive the world, but they are actually one, meaningless without each other. Without motion through space, there would be no time. Stripped down to its most abstract, theoretical meaning, sustainability ultimately slides along one scale only, the space-time continuum. But in practical terms, there are innumerable scales, from the microscopic to the cosmic, depending on your point of view.

Cougars represent one end of the landscape spectrum of scales in their requirements for large regions of forested habitat connected to other large, forested regions. At the other end are soil organisms, which need tiny, precise microsites. Soil is the foundation of ecosystem wealth. As the medium for plant growth, which then fuels all animals either directly or indirectly, soil ultimately defines the biological contours of sustainability. That's why acid rain, which leaches essential nutrients from the soil, is so dangerous. Some areas in the Appalachians have already been so degraded by acid rain that they have lost the capacity to regrow another forest.

Between these two ends of landscape spectrum are birds. Various associations or guilds of birds reflect significant habitat differences. There are birds of urban and agricultural areas; birds of streams, ponds, marshes, and lakes; birds of edges along forests, fields, streams, and developed areas; and birds of the forest interior. Other guilds are composed of birds that migrate for the seasons, binding whole continents together, and birds that stay in a few acres of home range year-round. Bird communities bring many scales together and serve as an index of ecological integrity.

Taken together, these three categories—carnivores, soil organisms, and birds—offer essential perspectives on the health of an ecosystem. On Doe Mountain, any cougars would be likely to benefit from the two clear-cuts, as long as those cuts remained embedded within deep forest, because of the increase and concentration of deer. Birds that use edges will also benefit for a couple of decades. Birds of the forest interior, whose numbers are rapidly dwindling due to habitat fragmentation, have lost a relatively small amount of habitat, which Britt figured should become available again in perhaps fifty years. But if a particular species of soil invertebrate lived only under the rocks in one corner of the clear-cuts, and the trampling of those rocks by logging killed every individual, then that species just ran out of luck.

Any attempt to balance all the scales teeters on a fulcrum of human knowledge. Britt checked with the state Natural Heritage program to ascertain whether any threatened or endangered species had been inventoried in the area. During timber cruises, he and his staff looked for any unusual or distinct natural features, like caves or bogs, which might signal ecological rarity. If found, historic sites like old homesteads or cemeteries would also have been noted and protected. No protocol exists to monitor soil organisms, though, so they were on their own.

Given the current state of knowledge, Britt felt that these clearcuts were appropriate use of a technique bitterly reviled by environmentalists but useful under particular conditions. He counted on natural processes to regenerate a native forest with no significant losses to the ecosystem.

Only the shattered rocks would forever mar the beauty of renewal.

---

Richard Cartwright Austin may be a Presbyterian minister and internationally known theologian, a high-brow intellectual and refined aesthete, but he's also something of a sybarite. I found this reassuring, in a man who might otherwise intimidate. What gave him away was his hot tub, set into a gracious deck with beds of summer flowers and a view into the Clinch River valley of southwest Virginia. It was an appropriate setting for a man who, in articles and an acclaimed series of books, urged a return to the sensuous as a way for Christians to reconnect with nature. By awakening the senses—to such everyday pleasures as the smell of a rose, the taste of a tart apple, the tingling of snow on your tongue—Dick believed that people would be more receptive to the experience of natural beauty. And it was in that human experience of beauty, with all its emotional, intellectual, spiritual, and cultural entanglements, that Dick saw the salvation of the world.

The sensual side of human nature has traditionally been suppressed under Christianity as a source of sin. In a similar vein, Christianity has also generally regarded nature as an enemy or a slave. Christianity has, in fact, been blamed for the current environmental crisis because of its espousal of a human right to dominate nature. Dick therefore sought to rearrange some of the building blocks of Christianity and fashion a Christian perspective of nature that would both strengthen the faith and enhance its moral beauty. Environmental ethics, he believed, would spring from the relationship that natural beauty engenders in those who perceive it. The observer and the object considered beautiful are no longer detached from each other but engage in a potentially meaningful relationship.

I played a lively game of object and observer with Dick's cat, who cleverly thrust a paw through a tear in a screen door every time I waggled my finger, while I waited for Dick to finish a phone call from Moscow. Although graying hair hinted at his recent retirement from professional church work, his mustache was still sandy, his blue eyes were unfaded, and his pace had hardly slackened. Since 1959, when he entered the ministry in the mountains of Pennsylvania, he had served at sixteen churches, most in rural settings, although some also in Washington, D.C.

Early in his career, he was contacted by a federal agency then called the Soil Conservation Service (now Natural Resources Conservation Service), which originated during the Dust Bowl years of the 1930s. "During the Dust Bowl, the Soil Conservation Service began trying to reach farmers through the churches," he said. "Most American theology dealing with care of the land is courtesy of the federal government. Only recently have churches begun to rethink their attitudes toward the environment."

Dick was one of the first clergy to take up the question of religion's relationship with the natural world. "I was a decade into my ministry before I realized that my Christian training had ignored both God's relationship to nature and the ethics of human relationships with the natural world," he said. His special ministry in faith and the environment intensified in the early 1970s, as he was finishing a five-year pastorate in West Virginia. As an organizer of resistance to strip mining, he felt called to a more direct approach to the relationship between faith and nature. He decided to become a farmer. He bought an old farm of 160 acres on the Clinch River. The house had been abandoned for twenty-five years when he moved in. It was a modest clapboard house with a gracious air. I ran my hand along the railing of the unusual curved porch and thought how hard it must have been to leave this house behind.

One of Dick's first mistakes was to take an extension agent's advice to clear a hillside of brush. The agent meant the unruly shrubs and vines that people often consider worthless and unattractive but which represent a natural stage in the process of reversion of clearings to forest. Afterward, erosion from the naked hillside filled Dick's pond. "Much of this mountain land should never have been cleared," he said, "and I learned to just let it grow back."

Like most old farms, Dick's had a large woodlot, in this case about a hundred acres. From early on, he saw that he had good timber. Is there a woodland owner who doesn't think about financial gain from the trees? Economic profit is the driving force of our economy, ourselves. It's a byword among foresters that woodlots must yield profits for their owners, otherwise what's the point of managing?

Dick was certainly interested in the profitability of his woods. But he was no more satisfied with the advice of the consulting forester he asked than with the extension agent's, and by then he was thinking twice about taking any of it. He saw the muddy streams and mangled woods left by conventional forestry at work around him and decided he wanted to do something different. He built a barn of his own lumber, cutting the trees himself and hauling them to the mill. There was no one else he trusted to cut responsibly. With his organizing skills, he galvanized interest in a new kind of forestry in southwest Virginia and helped found a regional nonprofit group named Appalachian Sustainable Development. In the process, Dick came to know and trust one of his neighbors as a skilled, low-impact logger. I was there to look at the timber cut they had completed the past autumn.

Dick's woods bordered a pasture, and just beyond the barbed wire fence we passed through an edge of thick, weedy brush before entering the woods proper. "It's unclear whether there can be such a thing as sustainable forestry," Dick said. "It has been a Holy Grail since Gifford Pinchot established the whole idea of forestry in the early twentieth century. Most of what's been done in its name has degraded the forest. We can't just assume that trees of the same quality or quantity will grow back where we've cut, because they haven't in many places. And it's getting tougher with increased acid rain and climate changes. No one has shown a sustainable forestry that I've seen, at least in this part of the country. It's ridiculous to call most of the forestry that is done today sustainable. Not a single logging job in southwest Virginia on private lands has even passed Best Management Practices standards in the eight years since the state adopted them."

Best Management Practices, called BMPs, are specific on-the-ground procedures that reduce environmental damage, particularly erosion. They consist of technical standards for roads, stream crossings, and log loading sites, all of which have far more potential for erosion than the logged area itself. Whether the use of BMPs should be required by law or left voluntary is at the heart of a raging debate over the public versus the private values of forests.

Until recently, when it came to woodlands lovely, dark, and deep, the direction of environmental concern was toward public lands. Government-owned lands usually provide for public input into the land use planning process. Private lands have no such formal mechanisms, and chance conversations between neighbors at the local store are increasingly unlikely as absentees and strangers buy forested lands. Legislation therefore offers the most immediate way to address practices, such as clear-cutting and road building, that can have destructive effects on water quality, wildlife habitat, and scenic beauty.

Legislation of private forestry is nothing new. Gifford Pinchot, whose name Dick had invoked, was America's first professional forester, and he strongly advocated federal control of cutting on private forestland. That hasn't happened, although some federal laws do affect forestry, particularly the Clear Air Act, Clean Water Act, Coastal Zone Management Act, Endangered Species Act, and various laws on wetlands and the use of pesticides and herbicides. For the most part, though, direct regulation of forestry has been left to the states. In the 1940s, some states began adopting "seed tree" laws that required reforestation to avert future timber famines. In the 1960s, a handful of states passed more comprehensive forest practices laws. After passage of the federal Water Pollution Control Act Amendments of 1972, most state forestry agencies began to develop BMPs.

BMPs differ in every state, but all focus on protecting soil from washing away and clogging the streams with sediment. One of their most fundamental features is the concept of streamside management zones. Of varying widths, but increasing to one hundred feet or more according to the size of the creek or river, these zones should be left undisturbed or only lightly harvested. Streams should be crossed at right angles with timber bridges or culverts. Water bars and dips are recommended for road drainage. All skid trails, the routes by which logs have been dragged to the trucks, and landings, the places where the logs are loaded onto the trucks, are to be seeded, fertilized, and mulched.

Most southern states have opposed the enactment of forestry laws and rely on voluntary use of BMPs. But as Dick pointed out, compliance is often very poor. An audit by the Virginia Department of Forestry completed shortly after my conversation with Dick found that only 17 percent of logging jobs across the state had properly implemented BMPs, although that was a significant increase from a similar audit six months earlier. Active or potential water quality problems existed on 62 percent of the sites. "The only thing that will make some people change," my own county forester told me, "is the law."

But the growth of what some foresters view as "government command-and-control bureaucracies" raises the hackles of quite a few landowners, not to mention most of the forest products industry. Forestry regulations challenge a particular idea about ourselves as Americans, an idea based erroneously on absolute rather than usufructuary rights to property. The "it's my land and I can do what I want" syndrome renders ecosystem management downright subversive. But do I have the right to crisscross my land with destructive logging roads, causing the creek to silt up with every hard rain? If I need money because I'm sick, should I be able to earn the most profit in the quickest way, regardless of the loss to future productivity?

Our ideas about property are still evolving. After all, it wasn't very long ago that human beings were bought and sold like livestock, and on the whole that didn't work out very well. A new social perspective is now emerging, one that focuses not on individual tracts and private rights, but on aggregates of land across political jurisdictions and on the responsibilities of landowners to the community and to the future.

One school of thought holds that most people want to do the right thing, if only they know what that is. Education of landowners, loggers, and forestry professionals offers a slower resolution than legislation, but one that protects property rights. Restructuring of capital gains and estate taxes to reward good stewardship would be another powerful nonregulatory route. Market-based incentives such as Smartwood certification, aimed at tapping the market of socially conscious consumers, constitute yet a third approach. These are slow ways of changing the culture toward a new land ethic.

But there is another school of thought that holds that private economic interests will usually prevail over other values unless laws safeguard the public interest. There is a certain urgency in the debate, as global demand for wood products rises. Coincidentally, many eastern forests are reaching economic maturity after the abusive, widespread logging in the early twentieth century. The proliferation of chip mills across the South, and the controversy over the large clear-cuts that they provoke, herald the clash between economic and ecological values. A lesson from forest ecology could be applied here: Diversity is good, because it enhances stability. A diversity of approaches, from education to incentives to regulation, offers the best support for the necessary change.

Change, at least its more drastic forms, was what Dick sought to defeat in his woodlot. He had made a thirty-thirty forestry rule for himself: to remove no more than 30 percent of the standing timber, so that thirty years in the future, the same species and ages that were there now would be there still, just not the same trees. He decided to cut about fifty trees over fifty acres after a big storm knocked down a number of prime specimens of red oaks, poplars, and ashes. His neighbor took them out with a mechanical skidder. "Now I know that someone can use conventional equipment and do a good job," Dick said. There was no bare ground in his woods that I could see, but a lush understory punctuated by an occasional stump. I stood on one that was three feet in diameter and surveyed the equally large poplars and ashes still remaining.

All BMPs had been followed but were hardly necessary because the disruption was so slight. Because the woods were more or less surrounded by farm fields, yielding easy access, no new roads had been made just for the timbering.

"It feels sustainable," Dick said, looking around. "I don't like the word stewardship; it treats nature as a thing, objectifies it. We need to develop a new moral relationship with nature. We are abusing the body of our Lord, not in a metaphysical sense, as pantheism holds, but in an ethical sense. I don't believe that self-restraint will be enough to form this new ethic and stop our overuse of natural resources. Love is the only motive sufficient to protect the world. The changes required of human society to give nature its due are so far-reaching and challenging, only love can induce them. If we come to protect the earth, it will only be because we have discovered a new delight in God through love of the beauty in nature. And in the image of God, we carry responsibility for life in the world. We have a vocation both to experience and to cultivate the beauty of the world."

I stepped down from my stump, feeling that Dick ought to have it. The beauty of the world was at the moment captured in the suffused green shimmer of late-summer sun on the canopy, which stirred now and again in a warm breeze. In his book *Beauty of the Lord,* Dick writes: "Beauty perceived in nature serves not so much to suggest higher truth as to indicate the value of the life and relationships perceived. . . . The beauty in life-giving relationships is heightened when these relationships support diversity and individuality or span distinctions between beings. Ecology may be a science of natural beauty, developing understanding of the relationships among beings in the natural order. Beauty reflects the health of life . . . its very absence can serve to warn us of problems."

The experience of beauty is real enough, but dangerously subjective or, as Dick put it, "corruptible." There can be no absolute standard of beauty, because our perceptions of nature are shaped by our culture, and in our urbanized culture, beauty is almost entirely based on one sense only: vision. Beauty may lie in the eye of the beholder, but we're all wearing corrective glasses.

Given a choice, many people find a domesticated, pastoral scene more beautiful than wild, uncontrolled, threatening nature. And examples abound of natural scenes that are considered beautiful but are corrupt: a pristine river in which every living thing has been killed by acid rain, grasses waving in the wind because the soil can no longer grow trees, a fiery sunset colored by air pollution. Visual beauty, Dick knew, is no guide to ecosystem health. Real beauty lies, rather, in actions that build life-sustaining relationships; moral rectitude then flows from those relationships. The philosophy may delve into murky depths, but the ethical lesson is clear: BMPs are beautiful.

––––––––––

To Harry Groot, the beauty of sustainable forestry lay in a phrase: value added. The term refers to the processing steps by which raw materials are converted into salable products, with each step refining the resource and thereby adding more value to it. Only when that processing is done within the human communities where resources are extracted can local residents expect to benefit in any significant way from the extraction. Like most people who attempt to define "sustainability," Harry believed that it must include human communities in the landscape.

Economic networks are therefore as important as ecological ones. All living communities have economies and budgets, but humans seem to be the only ones that use money. Money tends to corrupt local economies against local ecologies by moving one crucial step away from barter. But this is drifting back toward philosophy, and practicality is what's ahead.

Harry could pass for a farmer, solid and grizzled, and for a logger, too, in his ball cap. He was both, as well as a mechanical engineer by training and a philosopher by instinct. He grew up mostly in West Virginia and worked in wood products from pulp to sawmills, for the federal government and private industry. In 1983, he and his wife, a schoolteacher, bought a 110-acre farm in southwestern Virginia to explore a different way of life. "We were leftovers from the 1970s," he said. "We wanted to go back to the land and help solve problems instead of making them."

In the 1990s, Harry worked for the Appalachian Regional Commission, the federal agency established during the 1960s' War on Poverty to develop southern Appalachia. His job was the transfer of technical information about wood products. He also worked as a consultant for structural analyses of timber frame building, a nailless technique of beams joined by dovetails. "I've had a lifelong interest in wooden things," he said.

Classical music played on the radio in Harry's timber frame shed, attached to his solar kiln. A sign on a lintel read: "We didn't inherit the land from our fathers; we're borrowing it from our children." After Harry had gotten fed up with state bureaucracy a couple years earlier, he decided to start his own logging and sawmill business as a separate entity from the organic chicken farm he also operated. To express his philosophical approach, he named his new company Next Generation Woods. Since he wasn't a professional forester, he advised his clients, who mostly owned less than fifty acres, that they should get one, but they rarely did. This is typical; most nonindustrial private forest owners don't hire a forester when they decide to log.

Harry works with landowners to select individually the trees to be taken. "Then comes the first unit of value added, namely the mill," Harry said, walking over to his portable Woodmizer just outside the shed. "More and more small equipment is becoming available now, especially from foreign manufacturers in Finland and Sweden, some in Germany and Italy. But Woodmizer is American. This is their top end, one of the biggest, with hydraulics and a computerized headrig." At one-sixteenth of an inch, the bandsaw kerf, or split made by a bandsaw, wasted much less wood than commercial mills, with circular saw kerfs of one-quarter to three-eighths of an inch. Plus Harry could pick and choose how to cut to maximize the lumber that each tree was capable of producing. A pile of scraps and sawdust testified to recent use. The scraps would become firewood; the sawdust, mulch.

After he allowed the sawn boards to air-dry for a while, Harry stacked them in the solar kiln with small wooden sticks called spacers to allow air circulation (he had tried putting boards straight into the kiln after milling and found that it took far too long). Kiln drying is a crucial second step in the value-added chain, because many wood product outlets will not buy lumber that is only air-dried. Air drying is slow and uneven, and boards often continue to warp and shrink even after they are nailed in place. This makes customers unhappy. Furniture makers and other craftsmen will use only kiln-dried wood. "Especially in a house with air-conditioning," Harry said, "wood will shrink if it's only air-dried."

From the side, the kiln was a large right triangle, eight feet at the base. It was twenty-four feet long and had a total capacity of six thousand board feet. From the front, the sheen of plastic turned it into a gleaming metal spaceship. Black plastic was used to absorb heat evenly and keep direct sunlight from drying some boards more quickly than others. Boards were dried to a final moisture content of 7 to 8 percent, the same as a conventional kiln.

"Solar drying is less controllable than electric," Harry said, "so commercial operators aren't interested. I sell mostly to a local market." Electricity is still necessary for the six small fans that drive air through vents in the lumber pile. "The electric bill runs around twenty dollars a month," Harry said. He was working on instrumentation that would allow for more precise control of air temperature and humidity. The kiln cost $2,500 to build, including the concrete floor and fans.

"The length of drying time depends on season, also species," Harry explained. "Poplar is fast, oak is slow." Ideally, he could put in six loads a year, at roughly eight weeks each. He stacked the dried boards in a storage shed nearby. Cherry boards were the most valuable, then walnut and red oak, then poplar and birch. "I'm not making any money," Harry said, "but then I'm not losing any either, just breaking even, although that's without paying myself any salary. Living in a rural community, folks always need low-grade boards for barns and sheds. Also, I'm often asked for substitutes for chemically preserved wood, like locust, which is naturally resistant. There's a big demand for that, one that I see driven to a large extent by women, for the sake of their kids."

Harry had helped design a larger kiln for the nonprofit group Appalachian Sustainable Development, which was established in 1995 in Abingdon, Virginia. One of many innovative forestry ventures across Appalachia, its goal is to bridge the gap between sustainable forestry and community development by adding value. Appalachian Sustainable Development purchases logs from forest owners on the open market, but only under management plans completed by the professional forester on its own staff. One bottleneck is finding loggers willing to work under ecological standards geared toward getting the organization certified under Smartwood. Milling is contracted out to small bandsaw owners like Harry, although purchase of the group's own mill is possible in the long term. The logistics of sawing on site and stacking immediately with spacers, which is labor-intensive but necessary to produce high-grade lumber, are still being worked out. Drying and storage sheds and a solar and wood-waste-fired kiln are nearly completed. Eventual capacity could reach three hundred thousand board feet a year.

The forester for Appalachian Sustainable Development figured that two hundred acres of woods per year would be enough to sustain operations. This was not likely to offer serious competition to the established mills in the ten-county region the group identified as its service area. The kiln-dried lumber would be marketed at a premium price as coming from well-managed forests, with much of that premium going back to landowners and loggers in the form of higher log prices. There is a growing demand for certified wood from secondary processors, such as furniture makers, and from builders and architects in the "green building" movement. Appalachian Sustainable Development is taking a brave new approach to value adding, but it still wasn't as far as Harry wanted to go.

Generally, logging jobs happen in one of two ways. In the most common scenario, a logger contacts a landowner and negotiates a percentage split on a timber harvest, based on receipts for the logs at a mill. Landowners are at a disadvantage if they don't know anything about their timber or if they don't have a clue about what logging could mean for the future of their forest. It's also easy for a logger to cheat a landowner with mill receipts. "In the two years I've been logging," Harry said, "every client has a logger horror story."

The other method is through sealed bids, a process based on a timber inventory and usually conducted by a forester working for a landowner. The forester can retain the right to reject all bids if they don't meet certain conditions, such as guaranteeing a minimum value, or implementation of BMPs. Landowners who use foresters for a timber sale usually get a better deal all the way around, as well they should, since that's what they're paying the forester for. But only a small percentage of forest owners use foresters, and as forest tracts become ever smaller, even fewer landowners are likely to. One hundred acres is sometimes given as a minimum size for effective timber management, but about 30 percent of the forests of the Southeast are held in smaller parcels, and the trend toward fragmentation is increasing.

Many of the new forest owners lack a rural background and are less willing to incur dramatic changes to their forests through harvesting. Even if they were, they would be hard-pressed to find an interested forester, because foresters, like loggers, are usually paid by a percentage of the sale. There is therefore little incentive to work for owners with small wood volumes.

Harry wanted to introduce an entirely different set of dynamics to timber sales, one that concentrated not on the marketing end of value adding, but on the supply end. He wanted to form a landowners' cooperative. We are not talking here about a simple association of landowners, of which dozens exist and do good works such as holding workshops and printing educational newsletters. No, by cooperative Harry meant neighboring landowners pooling their timber assets into an economic force to be reckoned with. The ecological forces they could muster wouldn't be too shabby either.

Co-op! The very word is suspect, with smarmy undertones of socialism. Cooperatives are economic enterprises that are owned and controlled by those who are doing the work, not by investors or their hired managers. They date back to at least the eighteenth century, when even in the early days of the Industrial Revolution, it became obvious that exploitation was the name of the game. Some of the first co-ops were organized by starving British weavers. Modern forms of cooperatives date from 1844, when a group of weavers in Rochdale, England, founded a mutual-aid society. The Rochdale principles include democratic control based on one member, one vote; nondiscriminatory membership; and distribution of net profits in proportion to patronage by the members. Supplemental guidelines emphasize using part of cooperative earnings to expand operations, reserving funds to cover depreciation and meet emergencies, and providing educational activities for members.

By their very nature, cooperatives cooperate, and there has been an International Co-operative Alliance since 1895. Its current membership runs to nearly a billion individuals in ninety-three countries and includes consumer, agricultural, fishery, housing, and credit cooperatives, among others. The greatest concentration of membership is in Europe.

Europe has a long and honorable tradition of socialism. Two-thirds of European forests are held in a large number of private hands, mostly rural families, with average holdings of about twenty acres. Forestry cooperatives are well established, especially in Scandinavian countries, and do everything from sharing machinery to lobbying politicians. Many European governments recognize cooperatives as a goal of national forest policy. In September 2000, the European Community sponsored a European Day of Family Forestry in Hanover, Germany. Participants issued many proclamations, one of which advocated even stronger self-help associations of forest owners.

Cooperatives have not found much fertile ground in America, where competition is red-blooded and cooperation is a sop for the weak. Agricultural cooperatives have had the most success. The National Grange, a cooperative for farmers, was founded in 1867 by the American agriculturist Oliver Hudson Kelley. In an explosion of enthusiasm, more than twenty thousand Granges at local, county, and state levels were organized in thirty-two states, drawing nearly a million members. Some Granges even tried to manufacture their own farm machinery. Most ventures collapsed quickly because of poor management and powerful private competition. By 1880, membership was barely over one hundred thousand—but a core persisted. Today the National Grange has about three hundred thousand members in thirty-seven states.

Forestry cooperatives were almost nonexistent in America until a sudden burst of interest in the 1990s. In less than a decade, a dozen or more co-ops sprouted up, especially in the upper Midwest. The ambitious Sustainable Woods Cooperative, based in Lone Rock, Wisconsin, soon became a model for Harry and others. Like Appalachian Sustainable Development, the Sustainable Woods Co-op had its own solar kilns and subcontracted out the milling. But it was taking a step further along the processing chain by producing finished hardwood products such as flooring, paneling, and siding. And the entire operation was owned by more than a hundred private landowners in eleven southwestern Wisconsin counties.

To raise operating capital, members pay an initial fee of $100 plus $2 per acre of natural forest owned, which for most members is between forty and eighty acres. Members are not required to sell their timber to the co-op, but if they choose to, they also buy market stock in proportion to the amount of their timber as an investment in the processing facilities. Profits are distributed in the same proportion. Certified under the Smartwood brand, the cooperative also provides professional forest management and educational services.

Much of the economic viability of the co-op and similar ventures depends on the willingness of consumers to pay a little more for certified products, willingness demonstrated so far mainly in European markets. The stakes are high: By controlling the entire value-added operation, the co-op figured it might eventually be able to multiply the value of a tree up to seventy times over conventional methods.

Sustainable Woods Co-op was the kind of setup that Harry had in mind, but he was finding it was hard going. Interest from the various people and groups he approached, even environmental groups, was wan. "People around here like being independent," he said. "Maybe the harsher weather in the Midwest fosters a more cooperative attitude." He had a shy smile.

So for the moment he was concentrating on writing newsletters and newspaper op-ed articles to build some interest in a forestry cooperative. And he was spending a lot of time in his own woodlot. Good farmers have always recognized the benefits of maintaining a healthy woodlot, and eighty acres of Harry's farm were well wooded. He had been cutting gradually and keeping records of everything he did. An Acadian flycatcher sang in a small opening that Harry had recently made in the canopy. He regretted it.

"I took too much," he said. "My goal is basically to have a continuous canopy. Still, there are natural events like big blowdowns that occasionally open up patches. I try to work on that same scale, to mimic nature."

Mostly what he did was thinning. In thinning lies the true art of forestry. The jargon defines various nuances of thinning—low thinning, crown thinning, crop tree release—but the basic idea is the same: Take out the lesser plants to favor the better ones. Just like weeding a garden, as foresters never fail to say. "We can argue about a tree being valuable other than for timber, of course," Harry said. "And there are criteria for leaving important habitat trees, like standing dead trees. But I do want to make a living. I just want to do it with minimum impact."

Most forms of thinning mimic nature by taking out the less vigorous trees that would eventually die anyway from suppression by the better growers; thinning just speeds up the process. But there's no way to mimic nature in dragging logs out of the woods to wherever they are loaded onto a truck. This activity, called skidding, can inflict nearly as much damage as cutting a road with a bulldozer. The bigger the piece of equipment, the more damage it's likely to do. Harry used a four-wheel-drive tractor equipped with a power-take-off-driven winch. This was something the average farmer was likely to have—an important consideration, since farmers have always been an important group of woodlot owners. Harry handled the tractor with considerable skill. The two usually overwhelming signs of the passage of heavy equipment—trees scraped and gouged, ground torn and gaping—were barely visible. Nonetheless, mechanized equipment, even as Harry used it, was not at the bottom of the impact scale.

# MINIMAL MEASURES

THE FAMOUSLY BEAUTIFUL HILLS OF FLOYD COUNTY, VIRGINIA, attracted hippies in the 1960s and '70s, New Agers in the 1980s and '90s, and most recently, Y2K wannabe refugees from Wall Street. But it wasn't the Blue Ridge vista that was framed in the picture window of Jason Rutledge's living room. Instead, the barn filled the view. This made sense, because the barn and the horses in it were the center of Jason's life. As a horse logger, Jason used animal power to reduce the disturbance of logging as low as one could go and still take trees out. Jason was, in many ways, a deeply romantic man, but not when it came to his business. "Logging with draft animals isn't a matter of romantic nostalgia," he said. "It's simply the best solution to many current forest problems."

Agreement is widespread and growing. Facilitated by the Internet, an old and nearly lost tradition is rising, so to speak, from the slashes. A search for "horse logging" can turn up not only home pages for horse loggers from Nova Scotia to Texas to Oregon, but also help-wanted ads from landowners seeking horse loggers across that same continental span. In addition, there are landowner guidelines for writing horse-logging contracts, feature stories in various newspapers about local horse loggers, a directory of horse loggers compiled by

*Rural Heritage* magazine, and the Draft Horse Resource support site, with a chat room where you are disqualified for "cussing or slapping the reins."

Jason is a national leader in this revival. Clean-cut and graying at the temples, with a hank of hair falling over his forehead to his glasses, he looks like a professor. There is a determined thrust to his jaw. He is given to staccato outbursts of passionate speech in a voice graveled by cigarettes. "Don't call me a logger," he said. "Conventional loggers are mere tools of industrial forest interests. To call me a logger diminishes the highly skilled work I do. I'm a biological woodsman." By redefining the terms as well as the practices of logging, Jason sought to remake the image of a much maligned occupation.

Picturesque horses contributed mightily to that new image. The Suffolk Punch breed that Jason preferred had been developed in medieval times for farm work. Nearly two dozen silky chestnut horses with big, brown eyes and thick, black tails inhabited the barn, which was exceptionally beautiful. Sited on a hilltop, upslope from the modest, earth-bermed house Jason had built to accompany it, the barn caught the first light in the morning. It was two stories, architecturally sophisticated but based on old designs, with a breezeway through the middle and concrete floors, equipment bays, and a tack room. Whole shelves were lined with ribbons and trophies that Jason had won in draft horse competitions. The hemlock he had used for exterior siding had weathered into a soft gray. It took Jason five years to build and was more finished than his house, which as yet had only a basement floor with kitchen, bath, and several bedrooms.

Jason had milled his own house beams and heated the place entirely with a wood stove that stood against a brick wall. A garlic braid hung from a beam, and quarts of home-canned tomatoes sat in an open cabinet. The walls were lined with photos of children and horses, often together. Outside, an electric wire marked off lush pasture two feet from the picture window. Several sets of equine eyes stared in as Jason prepared for a day of logging. As he often did, he started the day with Vitamin I—that is to say, ibuprofen.

"I hurt all over," he groaned as he laced up his boots.

Biological woodsmanship is a physically taxing line of work, not to mention one of the most dangerous jobs around, and Jason had been doing it for more decades than he cared to enumerate. He was born in central Virginia and raised by his grandfather, who share-cropped tobacco with horses. Jason joined the service after high school and served in Vietnam. Afterward, he traveled around for a year or two on a motorcycle. Along the way, he was captivated by the fertile, rolling hills of Floyd County, and by 1983, he had scraped up enough money to buy eighty acres, much of which had just been clear-cut. He raised a family, eventually, of four children. He was looking for self-sufficiency, independence, and a job outdoors.

"But I saw that agriculture was not the way to go," he said. "Food is a giveaway. The system destroys farmers to keep food cheap. I had to find a way to live in the country without being destroyed. Turning to the forest was the obvious thing to do. This is a forested land. And I knew from experience what horses could offer. I've had a lifelong connection with horses. The human culture of draft animals is not something to be lightly discarded."

The horses were loaded into a trailer behind a pickup driven by Jason's son, Jagger. Jason had chosen the name because it was a medieval term for the keeper of the horses. Jagger had just turned twenty and was taking a break from college to work for his father. A champion wrestler, he was strong and lithe. He worried about his father. "Dad's getting too old for this. He doesn't even take Father's Day off, because that's Open Woods Day, one of his public demonstrations," Jagger said.

I rode with Jason high up in the seat of his log truck. The license plates read "HOSS LOG." It was noisy in the cab, and the break at a gas station was welcome. Jason seemed apologetic about having to get gas; he hated to buy it because it made him dependent on a far distant, politically manipulated product, and because his truck got only six miles to the gallon. Horses could haul the logs out of the woods, but getting them to a mill was a job for a truck. Jason had made a mitigating rule for himself: He would stay within a harvesting radius of ten miles from home. Today's job was nine on the nose.

Jason hitched his team, the ponderous but placid Skidder and Wedge, to a one-seat carriage, which he rode up a slope into a wood-lot that an absentee owner had hired him to log. Four of us followed him on five pairs of feet. Jagger and I walked together, talking about the forest. Behind us, Todd Buchanan led his horse, Dan.

Todd had arrived a month earlier as Jason's apprentice. He was several years older than Jagger and didn't talk much. I quickly learned to listen when he did, and not only because of his classic Appalachian dialect. Todd was from Mount Mitchell in North Carolina, the high-est mountain in the East. He grew up on a farm that his family had owned for 150 years. He was very tall and skinny, with a trim beard and a clean-shaven head, which was usually hidden under a cowboy hat. Beneath the hat brim, his eyes shone a clear and piercing blue. Tattoos chased his arms up into his rolled-up sleeves. Todd lived in the tack room of the barn and swapped horse maintenance for instruc-tion. "I bear witness to Jason's mentoring," he said. "Not just of me, but several others I know personally."

Todd was one of many students that Jason had taught over the years in an earn-as-you-learn program. It wasn't easy to become a horse logger. Most of the two to ten thousand estimated horse loggers in the United States had learned from their fathers or grandfathers and were themselves nearing retirement age. Videos and manuals are avail-able, but it's not the kind of job you learn from books.

Occasional workshops are held around the country, but the most formal education is available in Canada, where horse logging is encouraged by governmental policy. In Ontario, Sir Sandford Fleming College offered a month-long field-based curriculum of silviculture, safety, and "equine technology." In British Columbia, where 94 percent of the land is owned by the provincial government, an amount of timber large enough to employ at least a dozen full-time loggers has been reserved for horse logging for ten to fifteen years.

Jason hoped eventually to offer a formal apprenticeship as part of the Healing Harvest Forest Foundation he had recently founded. With support from a board of directors and a membership base, he hoped to give his message more carrying power. His message was restoration forestry. "The forest is in a declining condition," he said. "Why should we want to sustain a forest that's been degraded by high grading?"

High grading has always been, and remains, one of the most popular harvesting methods. Only the valuable trees—that is, those most likely to be graded as high value by the mill—are removed each time the woods are cut. Diameter-limit cutting, which takes only trees larger than a certain number of inches in diameter, is a new term for essentially the same technique as high grading.

High grading means loggers don't waste their time on low-value timber, and it leaves the appearance of a functioning forest. Appearance is becoming an important aspect of forestry, because the new breed of landowner values aesthetics. The people who are buying those ever-smaller tracts of forestland tend to be better educated and more environmentally savvy than previous generations of owners. These new landowners are making different demands on the forest, demands grossly lumped together as "nontimber products." Beauty, the perpetuation of native flora and fauna, and clean water rank high on the long roster of nontimber products.

The most insidious feature of high grading is that it seems to leave all these qualities intact. But what high grading and diameter-limit cutting actually leave behind are the least valuable species to serve as seed sources, diseased trees that can spread infection, and poorly formed or damaged specimens that crowd out better trees. Repeated over a century and more, high grading has left low-quality timberlands across Appalachia and much of the East.

"The first step to sustainable forestry," Jason said, "is restoration forestry. Extraction is inevitable, and necessary for society, but our mission must be to maintain the forest not only intact, but in improving health." Through a self-directed program of reading from the most progressive forestry literature, and through his own experiences over thirty years, he developed a set of operating rules to correct the legacy of high grading. With his usual sense of word play, he called it "worst first," a term later picked up by other groups in the sustainable forestry movement; it's also called low grading. Jason liked to call it "tree gardening."

By any name, it's a form of thinning. It harvests the lowest- rather than the highest-value trees, in cycles of ten to thirty years. Jason composed a "perpetual management" contract with landowners that gives him first rights to log the same woodlot in the next cycle. That way, he stood a chance of realizing the benefits of his earlier delayed gratification; or if not him, his family business.

"What you leave in the woods is more important than what you take," he said, "because what you leave determines the future of that forest. I know I'll never live to see the results of what I do, but I'll be leaving a true living legacy to landowners of the future. Because by improving the forest, low grading is a wealth-creating management approach."

An example of just how quickly that wealth could grow lay on Jason's coffee table: a cross section of a poplar tree he had cut in his own woodlot seven years after he had thinned around it. The annual growth ring that represented the year of thinning was marked. In the seven years afterward, the tree's growth rate increased by 300 percent. This was not unusual; many studies document the dramatic power of thinning.

The morning silence was broken by chain saws as Jagger and Todd began cutting. I was glad for the warmth of my hard hat, because the day was cold even though it was spring, one of those days when you listen for birdsong but hear instead the dying snarl of winter in the wind. Still, on my list of Beautiful Woodlots I Have Known, this one ranked high. Jason had found rock piles and figured it was all cleared pasture a century ago, but the past was impossible to conjure in that luxuriantly leafy forest. There had clearly been little harvesting here for many years.

Mountain laurel was blooming, great, heavy, pinkish white bouquets of it. There were many features of old growth. Layers of vegetation formed a green haze from the ground to the tree canopy. Trees were of all sizes, from saplings to boles three feet in diameter. Lots of dead and downed wood littered the ground. The horses picked delicately through it with feet the size of buckets. Jason dismounted and flipped the reins around a bush, leaving his team to slobber quietly over it as he pointed out harvesting decisions he had made.

We passed a chicken-of-the-woods mushroom with salmon-colored flesh, part of which Jason had consumed last night for supper. Nearby was a huge scarlet oak stump. "I cut this one because scarlet oak is a short-lived tree, and once it's mature it's likely to blow down," he said. "But I found this one was still growing good growth rings, so I'll leave other scarlet oaks on this same contour. Those big, nice dominant red and black oaks, they're nicely spaced, so I left them. That black oak has frost cracks but they're not weeping, so it's likely to keep growing well until the next cycle of harvest. My approach imitates nature by preying on the old, diseased, or weaker victims. Just as the wild predators do, so should the harvesters of trees. This insures the survival and reproduction of the strongest specimens."

Jason selected his victims according to "nature's own tree-marking paint," or list of warning symptoms. He was working on assigning numerical values to each indicator to establish a "readiness for harvest" scale, but in general, a tree had to show at least three of the following signs: frost cracks, crown damage, butt swelling, festering wounds, or certain species of fungi and other diseases or insect pests, especially exotic pests such as gypsy moth and hemlock woolly adelgid. "There's fifty million board feet of hemlock in a ten-mile radius about to die due to the adelgid," Jason said.

Along with acid rain, certain pests and diseases introduced from other continents are a looming threat to forest health, because they can overwhelm an ecosystem that has never evolved any means to check their population growth. Chestnut blight is the classic example. Jason therefore cut alien invader species like the tree of heaven *(Ailanthus altissima),* even through there was no market for them.

Jason also cut some trees based on their species alone. "Some low-value species have become unnaturally dominant due to human intervention," he said. "Examples are red maple, hickory, black gum, scarlet oak, post oak, black oak, black birch, and beech. But I take only thirty percent of the canopy. I leave a perpetual partial climax. And I leave obvious wildlife features, like standing dead trees. Plenty of diverse habitat remains. At the same time, I also admit some sunlight to the forest floor for natural regeneration by seedlings, without prompting epicormic branching." Epicormic refers to buds stimulated by sun on a tree trunk, producing branches that disfigure the potential lumber.

Plenty of foresters disagreed with Jason's logic. In fact, selective methods (called selection harvesting) are rejected by much of the forestry establishment. Many of the more valuable timber species—yellow poplar, black cherry, ash, and many types of oaks—are generally intolerant of shade and require direct sunlight for seeds to sprout and thrive. The regeneration of oaks in particular—whose acorns have become an essential source of wildlife food since the demise of the chestnut—has been much debated. Clear-cutting has been justified vociferously as the only way to regenerate oaks.

Yet oaks were prominent in the eastern woods long before European settlers had a chance to clear-cut them. The abundance of oaks, and the even greater abundance of chestnut trees, may have been due in part to fires set by Native Americans. The extent to which Indians used fire for land management has been a topic of controversy for many years. Oaks and chestnuts have thick bark and deep roots that resist fires that kill off more vulnerable species. For the most part, fires of the pre-European settlement era, whether set by lightning or by Indians, were likely to have been burns of low to medium intensity. Such fires, as well as other disturbances like windthrow and insect infestations, would have resulted in relatively small openings along the scale of those that Jason created.

Jason was used to criticism. He saw himself as a burr under the saddle of the system, an iconoclast who was not always welcomed even by environmentalists, with whom he competed for grants. "This is a time," he said, "when wrong looks right because there's so much of it." He had visited the Menominee Tribal Forest in Wisconsin, perhaps the oldest example of sustainable forestry in the United States. The tribe has been harvesting its 220,000-acre forest since 1854 and processing the harvest in its own sawmill since 1908. Timber is carefully selected for harvesting from one end of the reservation to the other in such a manner that when the end of the forest is reached, the beginning is ready for cutting again. After a century and a half, and more than 2.25 billion board feet of harvest, there was more standing sawtimber volume in the forest than there had been in 1854. In 1995, Menominee Tribal Enterprises was one of the first to be certified by Smartwood.

Jason had also studied the Pioneer Forest in the Missouri Ozarks, an example of selection harvesting in an oak-hickory forest similar to those in southern Appalachia. Pioneer Forest is composed of 160,000 acres that private businessman Leo Drey began to purchase in 1954. Drey wanted to demonstrate that better forestry than the kind conventionally practiced would produce lasting and economically beneficial results. Single-tree harvests that left the best trees to grow even better have been the only method used. Even conventional foresters have acknowledged that the result is a productive forest of mixed oaks.

Jason believed oaks would also survive under his system. "One of the biggest reasons foresters today have trouble regenerating oaks is because clear-cuts congregate deer, who love to eat oak sprouts. My cuts don't stimulate enough browse to attract deer."

If deer don't kill the sprouts that grow from stumps, the eventual result is multiple-stemmed trees that have good root systems but are often weak in other respects. Jason left only the straightest, best stem. It was a real test of felling ability to avoid damaging that residual trunk. "Directional felling using the hinge and latch method takes real expertise," Jason said. "The point is to cut a tree first with the safety of the feller in mind, and second with minimal damage to other trees."

There was a loud crack, and a tree thudded behind us. "Damn that wind," Jason said. The whole time we'd been talking, he'd kept an ear cocked to the pitches and whines of the chain saws, interrupting himself now and again to check on things. "It's getting too windy," he called out now to Jagger and Todd. "Time to quit cutting."

Jagger packed up the saws, and Jason and Todd began speaking in low voices to their horses. Todd had been whispering to Dan off and on all morning, their heads tilting together, whenever he stopped to refill his saw. Now he and Jason maneuvered their horses into position to pull the downed logs. Todd called Dan the Miracle Horse, because he had learned voice commands in a matter of hours. "He wants to do what you want him to," Todd said.

Jason murmured a command, and his team leaned into the weight of three poplar logs. Following them, I measured the ruts they left: exactly one and a half inches deep. Although the crew had been working here for weeks, few trees showed any scuffs from the passage of horses and logs. Studies have found that mechanized skidders, which are much heavier and less maneuverable than horses, require wider trails, leave deeper ruts, compact the surrounding soil significantly more, and wound many more residual trees than horse loggers. Plus, they're noisy, smoky, and reek of diesel fuel instead of hay-filled barns.

"Don't be fooled, though," Jason cautioned. "Horse logging can be environmentally damaging, too, depending on the logger. Horse loggers can high grade as easily as anyone. And not all of them use the arch." This was not an arch at all, but a flat metal bar cantilevered fourteen degrees forward in front of the centerline of the cart axle. Notches along its length held the chains that are cinched around the front of a log. After years of research, Jason had adopted a design by old-time horse logger Charlie Fisher in Andover, Ohio. The arch hoists each log high enough to avoid gouging the ground as it is pulled forward.

Todd didn't have an arch yet. Without it, he and Dan left a noticeably deeper rut pulling one log than Jason had with three. Todd kicked twigs and forest duff into it. Jason taught erosion control through water diversion by piling up cull logs and brush, rather than by digging ditches or seeding. He didn't like to plant grasses, as was commonly done on skid trails, because most seeds available tended to be non-native plants. There were non-native grass seeds in the horses' manure too, but Jason was resigned to having little control over that.

Todd hoped to buy a second horse and a rig like Jason's by the end of the summer and move out on his own. Logging was the only life he knew. His father had been a logger, and Todd went to work helping him at age twelve, carrying gas and water and chains. A few years later, his father committed suicide. Todd went to work full-time at the local mill. Later he spent eighteen months in jail for a (nonfatal) shooting match with his stepfather over the sale of the family farm.

"I have a little problem with anger," he said.

He got the tattoos in prison. "When I first came to Jason's, I wore long-sleeved shirts and it was like to kill me, it was so hot. It was good to find I could relax and they didn't mind." He was letting Dan rest between the short, intense bursts of activity in which they were curling a log around a stump to angle it toward the path to the loader. A good, big log could weigh as much as Dan himself, at seventeen hundred pounds, or even more. Todd was careful to stay out of its way as it moved. He claimed two broken hips and one leg, plus cuts on most of his fingers and other body parts, incurred not as a horse logger, but before. He had worked for Georgia Pacific and Westvaco and other big timbering companies in various states. He married but divorced after Hurricane Hugo took him to South Carolina for many weeks to salvage storm-damaged timber and his wife found somebody else.

"I've done lots of clear-cutting and operated most kinds of logging equipment, including the kind with air-conditioned cabs," he said. "What I'm doing with Jason is backwards from what I've done all my life. This is the first time I've learned anything in ten years."

He had been looking for a way to log the small wooded lots owned by "snowbirds," the affluent retirees who summered in the mountains of North Carolina and wintered in Florida, when he heard about horse logging. He tried it first with mules. "After six months, I decided that mules required more knowledge than I had," he said. Then he learned about Jason and began working with Dan.

"I've gotten more enjoyment from Dan than any piece of equipment I ever had," Todd said. "No bulldozer has ever nuzzled me."

Todd had purchased Dan for $1,200 and was budgeting $50 a month upkeep and $100 to shoe him in the near future. At four years old, Dan had twenty more years to work. Todd was counting on it. He had been buying bits and pieces of equipment all spring and was down to his last $150. But there was hope on the horizon in the form of a potential job. It sounded perfect: eighty-six acres of woods much like this, not far away, where he could set up a camper or a trailer, build a little horse shed, and spend three years logging.

"I like to work," Todd said. "I like to see what I've done. It would be so nice being out there, day after day, working in the woods on my own schedule, able to get out early before it got hot." His yearning was palpable. As it happened, I had arrived in the middle of Jason's business negotiations for this job for Todd and had been invited to join all parties concerned for supper that night at the Blue Ridge Restaurant in Floyd.

Todd turned back to Dan. So far they had pulled three logs in to the landing, where Jason was loading them onto the big truck with the 1978 knuckleboom loader he had bought used. He preferred knucklebooms to wheeled loaders because they stayed in one place and didn't tear up and compact the soil all around the landing area. This fourth log would be Todd and Dan's last pull for the day. Todd moved into position behind Dan, ready to give the command to pull, but first he glanced over at me with a grin. "This is the hillbilly definition of sustainability," he said. "I'm going so slow I'll never get done."

There is an intimate relationship between low impact and slow production. Mechanized logging produces three to five times as much per day as horse logging. The average horse logger can produce one thousand to three thousand board feet daily, depending on topography (horses can handle most landscapes except steep slopes and rocky ground), skidding distances, type and condition of trees, and size of crew. A survey in Alabama of about fifty horse loggers found that most crews consisted of three people or less, who were usually family members. Logs were loaded onto trucks, most with homemade side-loading capabilities, and driven to the mill at the end of the day. The Extension Service forester at Auburn University who helped direct the survey calculated production in terms of weight rather than volume, and figured that each crew produced an annual average of sixty-five hundred tons of wood.

Markets are wildly variable, but if a mill pays an average of 30 cents a board foot, for example, on less-than-best eastern hardwoods, then thirty acres of them at fifteen hundred board feet an acre could net $13,500. It's common practice for conventional mechanized loggers to take around half of what the mill pays, while the landowner gets the rest, so long as no forestry consultant is involved, which is often the case. Horse loggers, however, generally require around 70 percent of the mill receipts, in order to provide a living wage over the longer time span needed to harvest. So landowners see less immediate cash, but they also see a forest that remains intact and is gaining future value. The best trees remain to grow higher-quality lumber at a faster rate, and wildlife habitat, water quality, and aesthetics remain at high levels.

There are other, less visible values of horse logging. More money stays in the local community, because horse loggers don't send off huge payments on equipment. Locally grown hay powers the skidders instead of fossil fuels. And as Jason pointed out, "You just don't go out to the barn one morning and find a baby skidder."

The percentage of horse-logged lumber in the wood products mainstream is still too tiny to measure, but even that much has triggered a hostile reaction from the conventional logging establishment. The American Pulpwood Association (now known as Forest Resources Association, Inc.) issued a technical paper claiming that any increase in horse logging would dramatically increase the threat that logging posed to water quality. Todd recalled that when he was in Idaho a few years earlier, the regular loggers felt resentful of horse loggers and wouldn't eat in the same restaurants. In Alabama, the survey conducted by the

Extension Forestry Service uncovered a fear among conventional loggers that horse logging would replace them completely.

That's hardly likely, especially on high-volume operations such as industrial pine plantations, but there is already more demand for horse logging than supply. Jason averages about a hundred acres a year, mostly by himself, and is booked up for years within his ten-mile-radius limit. Plus, he has more than enough previous customers to take him into two more rotations. "That's why I need to teach people like Todd, to carry on the cultural practices," he said. But, Jason had been asking himself recently, was it worth it?

Horse logging is not very profitable. "Nobody cares about loggers," Jason said. "Society is not very good to any of its workers at the bottom of the extraction scale." The median hourly wage of a logger in the United States is $11.65. Jason had never earned enough to finish the first floor of his house. "We have to be careful in the jobs we pick," he said, "because we can't afford to apply worst-first forestry on the places that need it the most. We have to choose woods that have at least some merchantable timber on the first cycle, because how can you do a worst-first harvest with low production and still be economically sustainable?"

In other words, who is going to pay for restoration forestry? Jason depended on landowners who could afford to be more concerned about the damage he wouldn't do than the money they wouldn't earn. So, like Harry Groot, Jason had come to the conclusion that as far as benefits to the local community were concerned, value added was the answer. He wanted his own sawmill, but Jason wanted a big one that could handle significant volumes of wood. What was stopping him was the lack of about $30,000 to buy a used one. He was bitterly disappointed when a grant he had been encouraged to apply for was awarded elsewhere. Searching for other options, he forged a partnership with Turman Lumber Company's Walker Mountain sawmill, about sixty miles away. Turman offered a bar-code service that could track individual logs through processing and sell them as sustainably harvested lumber under Jason's own product name, Draftwood.

"It would cost me thousands of dollars to get certified by Smart-wood," Jason said. "I can't afford that. Certification is just another extractive force in Appalachia."

Jason explained all this to me on the ride from the woods back to his house. It was late in the afternoon, and he hurried off to pick up his nine-year-old daughter, Ashley, from basketball camp. Todd quickly stabled the horses and got cleaned up for supper, but before we left for the restaurant, he wanted to show me something. With him on his travels, he carried a logging chain, with swivels, that he figured was maybe two hundred years old. The metal of the big, fat links was pitted and worn. In a reverent voice, Todd explained how it worked with a set of spreads or a spreader stick. "I got it from the great-granddaddy of my last employer," he said. "I have always liked to sit and listen to old men talk."

When we arrived at the restaurant, the only person in it was a woman of a certain age (namely, my own), but exceedingly well preserved and glamorous, with blond-streaked hair and blue eyes. This was Nancy, an acquaintance of Jason's and the owner of the woodlot to be logged. Nancy was tanned, fit, and fashionable in a body stocking with a vest over it and a long blue-jeans skirt over boots. "Do you mind if I smoke?" she asked and smiled gratefully when, trying to be gracious, I merely shrugged instead of grimaced.

The specials of the day were rib-eye steak and chicken and vegetables. The waitress was a polite young woman with fluffy hair of an indeterminate pale color. I ordered the veggies only, which, as expected, consisted of canned beans and corn, but also a delicious, homemade apricot salad of cottage cheese, Cool Whip, and canned apricots. Jason ordered the chicken, and Todd ordered the steak with a baked potato.

"I'd like two pieces of lightly toasted rye with two slices of tomatoes, one slice of onion, and nothing else, if you don't mind," Nancy said. "And I mean nothing, now," she added, laughing, as if all of Appalachian culture might be a conspiracy to slather her toast with fatty substances. "Absolutely no mayonnaise!"

The waitress went to the back of the restaurant and consulted in whispers with another waitress, then walked back to Todd.

"I'm sorry, but there's no potatoes," she told him. They settled on rice. Nancy had begun to describe her interest in macrobiotic diets and water shiatsu when the waitress came back again.

"I hate to keep bothering you," she said to Todd. "Do you want a large rib-eye or a small one?"

"Biggest one you got," Todd answered. He was wearing his cowboy hat and a black-and-red–checked shirt with the sleeves rolled up. Indian maidens and horses glowed luridly on his forearms. I asked Nancy if she lived on the woodlot.

"No," she said, "I have a house on a smaller tract not far from it." She had moved there from California, where she owned, among other properties, a mobile-home park. Low-income housing was something she knew about, and a friend had told her there might be HUD money available. She wanted to build rental houses for poor people on her woodlot.

"This would be a chance to do more than just forestry," she said. "I want to take a holistic approach. Jason will supervise logging the white pines and getting boards milled. Did you ever read *The Good Life* by the Nearings? I'll do concrete slipforms instead of rock walls like they did, using the white pine boards. I can use the bark for landscaping mulch." She smiled at me, clearly very pleased about our little get-together. "It's just so wonderful to be a part of this experience. All the people are coming together; how could I pass it up? The best part is that I don't have to have anything to do with Todd. Jason will handle Todd."

Todd, who was sitting next to her, gazed into the middle distance somewhere beyond us. Nancy had a notebook open in front of her with a list of business details she wanted to go over with Jason: Why Todd would need his own liability insurance; how he should dispose of his trash from whatever accommodations he moved onto her property; the issue of her privacy ("I want," she said, "to state explicitly that this is a work relationship"); and her desire to keep visitors, drinking, and music at low levels.

"I been listening to chain saws," Todd volunteered in a low voice. "Quiet is nice."

"Now let me make sure I've got this straight," I said, slightly befuddled by the beer I'd had before dinner and fearful that I was missing some crucial element of logic. "You want to build concrete houses in a woodlot?" The ultimate destination of the white pine boards, once the concrete had set in the forms and the boards could be pulled away, would be the landfill.

"Oh, but," Nancy said, grasping the point immediately, "there wouldn't be enough lumber for houses!"

"There's enough for at least six or eight houses," Jason muttered.

"They'll be green structures that are healthy for people to live in," Nancy continued, blithely ignoring him. "They'll rise organically out of the mountain." The image of concrete houses like squat, square mushrooms rose up in my mind, sickly white, the kind that grow on dead wood, the very substance of decay.

The waitress came to check on us. "This toast is really excellent, you are a very good cook!" Nancy said extravagantly. The waitress smiled wanly and retreated quickly.

"Daddy, these beans and corn aren't as good as ours," Ashley complained. "Do I have to eat them to get dessert?"

"I know, honey, they're not as good as our homegrown, but yes, you have to eat them," Jason said. To my utter amazement, she did, and then sadly declined dessert because she was too full.

The conversation roamed from Nancy's building permit—she had one, but the total number of houses allowed seemed to be unclear— to her potential use of the logging trails for horse paths. She owned several horses and liked to ride. Making paths out of the skid trails left by logging was something landowners often liked to do, Jason noted.

The restaurant closed at eight o'clock, and the waitress looked unmistakably relieved when we rose from the table at about ten minutes till. By the time Jason, Todd, Ashley, and I squeezed into the pickup, it was nearly full dark. The wind had not died and was bowing trees over the road. Jason was infuriated over the philosophical contradictions in

Nancy's plan. "She's just too flaky to do business with," he growled. Plus, he was insulted at her flippant disregard of his attempt to steer her toward building with wood rather than concrete. Todd was talking softly to Ashley, who had climbed on his lap in preference to mine. She squealed with delight as he wrinkled his nose to imitate a rabbit. By the time we arrived home, she was asleep in his arms.

But there is no happy ending to this story. When the job with Nancy didn't work out, Todd began drinking more heavily, a habit that had already been noticeable. "He turned mean and belligerent," Jason said, "and we had to ask him to leave." Jason later helped him get a logging job, but Todd became involved in the theft of a trailer from a church camp next door to Jason's house, apparently to use at the job. "He trashed my name in this community," Jason fumed. "He was the worst experience I've ever had with an apprentice. From now on, anyone with more than two tattoos is going to need just as many references!" Todd disappeared, whereabouts unknown. He left Dan behind.

———

The healing power of the woods, which is perhaps their deepest level of beauty, might be said to reside in ginseng. The roots of this shadowy perennial have been so valued as a source of pure wellness that at times they've been worth their weight in gold. Even today, properly dried wild ginseng roots can bring many hundreds of dollars a pound, making it the most lucrative of nontimber forest products, although far from the only one.

The phrase "nontimber forest products" entered the language of forestry in the 1990s, when the yews of the Pacific Northwest went from being trash trees to sources of taxol, a cancer-fighting substance. Suddenly, foresters realized that many nontimber products represented tens of millions of dollars in annual sales. Several forestry schools initiated research projects, notably Virginia Polytechnic Institute's Department of Wood Science and Forest Products. Faculty there began investigating how nontimber forest products might be used as tools for sustainable community development.

The diversity of the Appalachian forest has always provided a wide spectrum of nontimber products that have a long tradition of personal and commercial consumption. Edibles such as ramps and mushrooms bring families and communities together in seasonal celebrations. There are hundreds of popular medicinal species besides ginseng, with goldenseal being the second most valuable. Many kinds of decorative floral products, such as conifer greenery and cones, grapevines, moss, and ferns, and landscaping products like azaleas and rhododendrons, are highly sought after. Special woods are required by artisans for carving sculptures and musical instruments. Walk into any health food store, florist's shop, or craft fair, and you're likely to find items harvested wild from the woods.

Of all these nontimber products, ginseng receives the most attention because it is so highly valued as a medicinal. And scientists have indeed found that ginseng may lower cholesterol, retard plaque in arteries, and stimulate the immune system. But usually you have to ingest it before you can tap ginseng's power. Sylvester Yunker first planted it, then spent a decade tending a garden of virtually wild ginseng on a woodlot bought for the purpose near Kentucky's Red River Gorge. In that magic place, the mere presence of ginseng not only buffered Syl's bitter past, but kept him so remarkably youthful that I took him to be fifty-five. He was seventy-two, and grinned to see the expression on my face when he told me so.

Syl has a full head of steel-colored hair, white mustache and goatee, pale blue eyes, and fair skin reddened by sun. He looks like a mountain patriarch, complete with snuff and a paper cup for spitting. He technically was not Appalachian, though, having been born and raised in Middletown, a village outside of Louisville.

"It was very rural at the time," he said. "We had only three acres, but Mother was a farmer; she had three hundred chickens. Behind our house there was seven hundred acres of woods. I grew up loving the woods; all five of us kids knew the woods. I was constantly in them; I'd get browned off at civilization, at my family in particular, and take off for days at a time. The first time I was six years old. I ate field corn from a neighbor's field and made a lean-to. But I didn't know ginseng then."

Syl made the acquaintance of ginseng in Korea when he was eighteen years old. He was in the army for two years right after World War II ended in 1945. As always, he looked to the woods. Because of the ancient forest that circled the globe when the continents were still one, several closely related species of ginseng are native to both North America and Asia. Medicinal use of the root in the mountains of Manchuria dates back five thousand years. The people of Asia believe that ginseng prolongs life by bringing all bodily systems into equilibrium. This is the essence of wellness.

"My interest was piqued right away as an eighteen-year-old in the Orient," Syl said. "I had a brother-in-law there also, an army captain who had been in China before the war. He was with a tobacco company, which taught the Chinese to grow tobacco. The government of South Korea grew tobacco and ginseng as monopolies and sold them to China. That's what financed the South Korean government. Later on, Mao Tse Tung closed the ports of China—he wanted to be self-sufficient instead of dependent on trade, but instantly a Chinese Mafia sprang up to black-market ginseng from Korea through Hong Kong."

When Syl came back from Korea, he went to law school, but in his last semester, he "had the honor of being the student who went the furthest at University of Kentucky before flunking out." He went back into the army in 1952 during the Korean War. He was a paratrooper, ranger, and pathfinder. In 1960, he went to Vietnam to advise Vietnamese paratroopers. "I came home in 1961 more or less in a basket," he said. "Today they call it post-traumatic stress disorder. It was diagnosed as schizophrenia then. That made it hard to get a job." His wife died ten years later, after a long illness.

Syl worked in insurance for a while through his father-in-law but became interested in environmental work. He went to California to study oil spill cleanup procedures and in 1970 started his own industrial cleanup company, "washing car shop floors, that kind of thing." He saved every penny he could to buy property.

"I've heard people in the ginseng business, both Chinese and American buyers, say that one-third of the world's people will give one-fifth of their income to have ginseng once a day," Syl said. "And that huge market has been historically stable, which is the first consideration of a long-term crop."

Ginseng has been one of the most significant crops of the Appalachian forest since the early 1700s. Through a worldwide correspondence network of Jesuit missionaries, a priest in Canada learned about ginseng's value in China and looked for a similar plant in the forest around him. He became the enterprising father of a market that quickly spread south along the North American frontier. Millions of pounds of dried roots were exported to Asia by American pioneers, especially Daniel Boone, who gathered tons of it. Some he surely dug from the Red River Gorge, which he traveled through in the late 1700s. As was his wont, to mark his passage Boone carved his name, not on a tree, but on a board he left in one of the gorge's biggest rock houses. Legend has it that he was asked toward the end of his life if he had ever been lost during his decades of exploring uncharted wilderness. "No," replied America's quintessential pioneer, "but I was plumb bewildered for a few days once." I bet it was at Red River Gorge.

A dendritic maze of red sandstone canyons, Red River Gorge would look like Utah if it weren't nearly swallowed by an exuberant forest. Beneath the canopy lies one of the greatest concentrations of natural arches in the world: more than a hundred in thirty square miles. Because the plateau into which the gorge is etched tops out at about thirteen hundred feet, there's little mountain chill. Hiking in summer can be a sweaty experience, as I found when I camped at the gorge in the Daniel Boone National Forest. The chill of a thunderstorm was a refreshing breath from heaven.

Yet a tropical ambience felt right. Big-leaf magnolias, reminiscent of banana trees but much larger, grew profusely across every tangled terrace. The abundance of pawpaws, whose fruit tastes like banana custard, amplified the effect. Rhododendron and laurel formed dense thickets of glossy green. Poison ivy vines grew so muscular that I mistook them for the outstretched arms of big oak trees. The rocks are cross-hatched, swirled, puckered, potholed, or sometimes as smooth as slickrock. On northern slopes, boulders are wrapped in a tight green Lycra of moss festooned with ferns.

It's hard to imagine loggers hauling out huge virgin logs from the gorge, but they did, about a century after Boone. They thought of it as a great adventure and a contribution to progress. Their faces peer out, inscrutable, from photos in historical displays. Still, they couldn't get every tree. In Clifty Wilderness, especially, trails still pass survivors of the old forest standing sentinel, hemlocks and poplars far beyond the measure of a human embrace. The mosquitoes just seemed that big.

By the time I met Syl, I was smeared with bug repellent. I was dressed head to toe with poison ivy and snakes in mind, because the gorge's snakes are as legendary as Boone. I figured I'd better be prepared for anything, because Syl was going to breach the cardinal rule of ginseng: secrecy. He was going to show me his ginseng patch.

Syl had searched for years before choosing this forty acres of old homestead not very far from the gorge, which was purchased by the U.S. Forest Service after the logging. He had studied the area where ginseng used to grow most abundantly in Asia and found that east-central Kentucky was almost identical to Xi'an province in China, 175 miles south and west of Beijing. "The parallel line that divides Kentucky and Tennessee runs right through Xi'an," he said, "and the weather is continental temperate in both. The topographical features are similar, too, with small mountains from the tip of North Korea south past Xi'an. The soil strata are sandstone and limestone and coal."

There was a coal seam on his property, a V-shaped trench behind the old homesite where the farm family had dug out chunks for home use. Syl's land had a cave; his neighbor's had an arch. The slopes were relatively gentle and lay with an east-northeastern exposure. The woods were young, having grown up since the farm was abandoned in 1943. This family, like so many others in the mountains, had moved to Detroit to work in steel factories during World War II. The house was gone, its wood reused elsewhere, but parts of the root cellar remained, and day lilies bloomed where Syl parked his camper for the summer. He had remarried and lived a couple hours away in Lexington. In the autumn, he planned to start building a house equipped with solar power. He had noticed how a ridge behind the old homesite made a protected microclimate and planted a fruit orchard and black walnut trees that were beginning to produce. The forest was maples, poplars, some hickories and ashes, bunches of cedars grouped here and there, and occasional pines. Under this canopy was a dense understory stirring in a warm, dry August wind.

"Ginseng keeps company with certain plants that can serve as indicators, like poison ivy," Syl said, using his planting stick to part the way through a menacing stand. "No, just joking. But stinging nettle, greenbrier, goldenseal, black cohosh, jack-in-the-pulpit, they'll all grow with ginseng. Those wild iris, now," he pointed across a tiny gorge toward a hillside of spiky green leaves, "ginseng doesn't like them. It doesn't like ferns, either, so I plant outside the fern drip lines." In wet weather, there would be a waterfall of thirty feet in that little gorge. Virginia creepers were abundant, always fooling my eye with their five leaves like ginseng.

But there was real ginseng, too. In fact, as my eye adapted to the suffused light, I saw that I was surrounded by the biggest, healthiest, most abundant ginseng I'd ever seen. Many plants bore flower clusters and green berries like flat peas. They all nodded slightly in the breeze, as if to acknowledge our presence. There was a small cliff behind us, and we faced into a pointillist canvas of greens.

"This is what the Chinese don't have," Syl said. "The reason they pay so much for American ginseng is that they've deforested their country and can't grow it wild anymore. Korea has a big business in cultivated ginseng, which is artificially shaded, fertilized, and sprayed with fungicides. But the fleshy roots that you get when it's grown like an agricultural crop are very different from the small, dark, rough and gnarly wild ones, with their concentric growth rings." Wild roots have been shown to contain stronger concentrations of the active ingredients in ginseng, which are conveniently lumped together under the name ginsenosides.

"Buyers can instantly discern the difference," Syl said. "That's why growing it virtually wild like this has such a potential market."

Wildness! Maybe that's what felt so subtly exciting here, this quiet thrill of being in the company of ginseng. There was a sense of wild forest life, as if cougars would find refuge in the cave on Syl's land. Red-eyed vireos warbled their incessant conversations without interruption. And yet this was unquestionably a value-added woodlot. Syl had managed to trace a fine line between wild and domesticated.

He demonstrated the planting stick he'd made: a Bowie knife with a strong blade taped to the end of a mop handle so that three or four inches of blade protruded. Also taped along the mop handle was a plastic pipe with a half-inch diameter. Syl plunged the blade into the earth, and if there was at least two inches of soil, he waggled the blade to make a V trench about three-quarters of an inch deep. Then he dropped the seed down the plastic pipe and stomped dirt over it. "Keeps you from bending down each time," he said.

And that was essentially all he did. Using seeds from his own plants, he seeded for five successive years in patches of one square yard. He spread the plants out enough to avoid mold, though, which is a big problem in ginseng plantations. So far, he had seeded four and a half acres, and planned to do ten acres total. The plants would seed themselves, too. "That way," Syl said, "roots of a multiplicity of ages, just like in the wild, will be available for digging every year, to thwart dealers who would say the roots are too uniform and therefore not wild."

Growing virtually wild ginseng is a companionable rather than a competitive endeavor. Syl's rule was never to weed or remove anything from the understory. His main forest management activity was to cut down the dead trees among his plants, because when they fell they often brought down neighboring trees, opening too big a gap.

Ginseng turns yellow and spotty in too much sun. Syl used the snags and other deadfalls to form terraces down some small ravines and slopes to hold forest litter and moisture. He also cut wild grapevines at shoulder height to prevent them from pulling down the canopy trees, but he left them growing so they might still produce grapes for birds. Here and there I spotted short pieces of black pipe half buried in the ground; these housed mousetraps. "Mice haven't proved a big problem," Syl said, "but voles are. Friends told me to leave Juicy Fruit chewing gum—chewed—in the vole holes, and you know, it seems to keep them away."

The ginseng plants below the limestone cliff were a deeper green and larger than the others. Ginseng likes calcium. "The plants reflect very small differences in conditions," Syl said, pointing out how some were larger or smaller because of soil or sun or nearby plants. Ginseng plants are sensitive, mysteriously so, disappearing for years for no apparent reason. Some plants have been known to go dormant for decades. Ginseng can grow for a century, its years countable as root scars, but the older it gets, the less robust its roots. "I think ten years is optimal, so that's how long I've waited to harvest," Syl said. "This fall I'll be digging my first roots. A ginseng grower has to be patient."

Plants are propagated from berries, which aren't produced until wild plants are at least five years old. Slow reproduction makes ginseng vulnerable to overharvest, just as dependence on natural forest makes it vulnerable to logging and fragmentation of habitat. With these strikes against it, wild ginseng in North America has a good chance of going the way of wild ginseng in Asia, where it has become extremely rare. An analysis of the American ginseng market by TRAFFIC North America, a wildlife trade monitoring operation, found that ginseng suffered from three major threats: habitat loss from logging and development, particularly in the southern Appalachians; a trend toward overcollection; and harvesting before plants or berries were mature.

A few months earlier, Syl had attended a conference hosted by the U.S. Fish and Wildlife Service to publicize a new federal law that made it illegal to export wild plants less than five years old. Big dealers had been invited so they could relay the information to their diggers. The dealers didn't like it. Syl explained how they were getting around the rule by asking their suppliers for a statement that the roots were grown, not taken from the wild. "But if you say, yes, these plants have grown from seed I've planted, they won't give you the price for wild roots."

Eight of the plants below the cliff were marked by numbered stakes. Syl had been taking photos of each of these plants every month or so. On plant number four, you could see significant growth from April to May. He later posted these photos and photos of the harvested roots on the Internet, hoping to cut out some middlemen. He got a few bids, but not as high as he wanted, which was $800 a pound. He knew that in Hong Kong, the price for wild American ginseng could go as high as $2,000 a pound.

Syl was challenging a trading network far older than the rules imposed on it. Commercial export of ginseng has been regulated only since 1975, when the plant was listed as a species of concern by the Convention on International Trade in Endangered Species of Wild Fauna and Flora (CITES). The U.S. Fish and Wildlife Service monitors wild ginseng based on annual harvest reports from about two dozen states. Ginseng exports more than tripled through the 1990s, to a peak of nearly 150,000 pounds and $32 million, but levels began to fall rapidly in the new millennium.

Eastern Kentucky supplies the largest single segment of the export market, averaging nearly thirty thousand pounds a year. West Virginia and Tennessee follow, with around twenty thousand pounds. Not coincidentally, these same areas of Appalachia contain some of the nation's poorest people. Ginseng hunting continues as a cultural tradition and an economic mainstay. Some families still dig ginseng, often from coal company lands, to buy clothes and books to send their children to school in the fall. When coal mines shut down, ginseng harvests go up, making it difficult to link harvest levels with estimates of plant populations. Between the closing of exhausted seams and the thorough mechanization of the industry, most mining jobs have dried up. Ginseng poaching is known to be worst where unemployment is high.

States have legislated varying rules to protect the plant, such as prohibiting harvest before the berries are ripe and requiring that harvesters properly plant the berries. Some national forests have established moratoriums on wild ginseng collection. Academic researchers are investigating the genetic viability of dwindling ginseng populations. It's thought that at least 170 plants are necessary to prevent inbreeding, but even these populations become susceptible as habitat is fragmented.

Stands of a couple hundred plants, if grown virtually wild from locally native seeds, could contribute significantly to ginseng conservation. Not only would they increase ginseng diversity, but they could also take pressure off wild stocks and make it economically viable to retain natural forest. The economic potential has attracted attention, not just from foresters, but from a variety of community activist groups. Several such organizations sponsored workshops where Syl taught his methods and provided starter seeds. Much of the interest in these workshops came from small farmers, often older people. "They're interested in something that will keep the young people at home," Syl said.

For Syl, the human community was part and parcel of ginseng growing. He started the Boone Sang Cooperative in his early years of planting, by publishing an invitation to a meeting in the local paper. Twenty-five to thirty people came. Half of them joined the co-op, hoping to pool their small, individual, eventual harvests into an amount big enough to attract a big exporter. Some were growing ginseng already; one was using artificial shade but stopped soon afterward.

Syl was also looking for ways to add value. He gave me a glass jar of ginseng conserve, which sold for $15. A blue ribbon held a handsome label: Kentucky Mountain Wild. Syl had handwritten the ingredients: Granny Smith apples, wild crab apples, wild blackberry, black walnut, honey, wild ginseng. Except for the Granny Smiths, they all came from his own woods. The jars were canned by a commercial kitchen in Rock Castle County. The ginseng amounted to one-eighth of an ounce. "At that rate," Syl said, "a grower could get five hundred dollars a pound."

Todd Lester in his home office near North Spring, WV, with a plaster cast of a cougar track that was confirmed by two independent wildlife experts.

Todd Lester with wife Jaquetta and daughter Shanda in Matewan, WV. Behind them, a plaque marks a bullethole remaining from the 1920 Matewan Massacre, the most famous incident of America's coal mine wars.

*Todd walks along a new road bulldozed for further development on coal company land where he saw a cougar.*

*Clear-cut above the road in a saddle of Doe Mountain, Giles County, VA.*

COURTESY OF BRITT BOUCHER, FORESTERS INC., BLACKSBURG, VA.

*Memorial to Devil Anse Hatfield in the Hatfield Family Cemetery in Sarah Ann, WV. Darkening on the head may be the result of acid rain from coal mined here and burned for electricity at power plants in the Midwest.*

*Two thirty-five-acre clear-cuts separated by trees left along the drainage between the cuts.* Courtesy of Britt Boucher, Foresters Inc., Blacksburg, VA.

*Harry Groot's solar kiln, attached to his open-sided work shed.*

*Harry Groot with his sawed and kiln-dried boards, ready for local sale.*

*Jason Rutledge logging with his team of Suffolk draft horses.*

*Jagger Rutledge spreads out logging debris to create water diversions on the skid trail and reduce erosion.*

*Dick Austin on his porch.*

*Todd Buchanan, veteran conventional logger and apprentice horse logger.*

*Syl Yunker and his ginseng planting stick.*

*Virtually wild ginseng planted in natural forest without tilling or weeding.*

*Marcia Bonta in her woods, which under her Forest Stewardship plan will not be logged but will function as a nature reserve.*

*Willamette Industries' Broad River Company Chip Mill at Union Mills, NC.*

*Rodney Robbins beside his burned sawmill.*

*Extensive clear-cutting in the vicinity of Union Mills, NC.* ONE OF MANY SUCH DOCUMENTARY AERIAL PHOTOS BY SUSAN F. LAPIS OF SOUTH WINGS, CHATTANOOGA, TN.

*Bill and Michael Best of Berea, KY, cutting tomato stakes on their portable Wood-Mizer sawmill.*

*The dining hall on the lake at Falling Creek Camp.*

*Blaine Puller, forest manager for Kane Hardwood, on a stump believed to have been cut by company founder T. D. Collins near Kane, PA, in the early twentieth century. Hay-scented ferns crowd around, forming a major obstacle to regeneration.*

*Kane Hardwood practices shelterwood cutting, in which fifty to one hundred trees per acre are left uncut, mostly in clumps to help protect against blowdown from wind.*

Mr. and Mrs. Don Hemphill boiling sorghum syrup into molasses.

Kane Hardwood has received both forest management and chain-of-custody certification from the Forest Stewardship Council. Each individual log must be tracked through the milling process to ensure that only logs from certified forests can be marketed as such.

*Ches Goodall hugs the biggest red spruce tree on his high-elevation acreage in VA.*

*The Kane Hardwood company house.*

*Ches Goodall examines a multiple-stem tree thinned by his brother Pen.*

*Mountaintop removal by Addington Enterprises, Inc., at the Star Fire Mine in Perry County, KY, has blasted away thousands of acres of natural landscape to leave artificial buttes and plains.* PHOTO BY JEFF L. LARKIN, UNIVERSITY OF KENTUCKY.

*Elk use sediment ponds to cool down on hot days.*

*Trees struggle to grow on mountaintop removal lands and usually die after about ten years because of compacted poor soil.*

*Mountaintop removal destroys 99.9 percent of native biodiversity and results in permanent grasslands and scrub, with occasional sediment ponds.*

*Large herds of elk brought to eastern Kentucky from Utah to graze the grasslands formed by mountaintop removal are magnificent, but do not represent a restoration project.* PHOTO BY JOHN J. COX, UNIVERSITY OF KENTUCKY.

When it came to marketing, Syl looked to tobacco as a model. Tobacco was one of the few crops left that small farmers could make money on, but it was under social siege. His first step was to develop a ginseng grading system to standardize root quality, in the way that tobacco leaves are graded. He compiled a bar graph of values by polling three hundred dealers, growers, and academics on questions of taste, smell, and visual appearance. It wasn't easy to get that information, though. His first fifty questionnaires elicited not a single response.

"Secrecy is ingrained in the system," Syl said. "It runs through the business, from diggers to the Mafia in Hong Kong. No one tells anyone anything. What finally did it for me was when I promised to send results of the poll to those that responded. Other people wanted to know, too."

What Syl ultimately had in mind was piggybacking the sale of virtually wild ginseng on the infrastructure of the tobacco industry. He wanted to cross-train tobacco graders to grade ginseng as well, and use the same warehouses and auction barns. He was also looking for markets for seeds, and he wanted to develop educational products like videos and other instructional materials. And then there was the entire domestic market to develop, with interest in herbal medicines expanding rapidly.

I had to ask. "Do you believe in ginseng?"

"I've used it," Syl said. "I saw 'tumor hospitals' when I traveled in China, and I knew the Chinese had always used it against tumors. So when I developed a bump on the back of my head that grew as big as my thumb tip, I started taking it. In two weeks, the bump shrank to almost nothing."

You can't argue with success.

I had another pressing question. "Why on earth are you so open about everything?"

"Secrecy has kept ginseng from being a recognized crop," Syl said. "Because of everybody being in the closet, its potential value is not known, and everyone wants to keep it that way. Dealers don't want diggers to know how much the Chinese pay, so they can keep their own prices low. Poachers do worry me long-range, though. The way most people protect ginseng is not to tell anyone."

Poaching is rampant. Its extent can be judged from conditions in two Appalachian national parks, where all collecting is prohibited. During the 1990s, nearly nine thousand poached roots were confiscated in Great Smoky Mountains National Park, and rangers were convinced they caught only a small percentage of illegal collectors. They took to sprinkling orange dye on wild roots to inhibit thieves, and even then they found scrubbed roots with particles of dye in dealers' bins. Shenandoah National Park successfully prosecuted a ginseng poacher in 1998 for stealing 178 roots, but the penalty was hardly proportionate to the potential profit of the crime: The man was fined $300, ordered to pay $162 in restitution, and placed on probation for two years, during which he was prohibited from entering the park.

"Some landowners are beginning to use GPS to document and locate their plants," Syl said. His idea of security was to come out of the closet. He figured that if he was out in the open, the community would become aware of the economic possibilities and would become protective of growers. "Landowners can see that if I'm successful, they might be too. I've only caught one set of poachers one time. I saw a strange car parked by the cemetery before my turnoff. Then, later, when I was working around the homesite, I heard a ginseng hoe hit a rock. I walked over with a 410 shotgun pointed at chest height. One of them had a revolver. I made them strip so I could check their pockets for roots. I got their IDs and saw who they were, then I walked them to their car. A couple days later, I stopped in to see the sheriff. He asked if I knew who they were. He said, 'Give me their names and I'll go talk to them.' I haven't had a problem since. Of course, if I had charged them, it would have come out in the paper, and then I might have had more poachers."

Being the antithesis of a thrill seeker, I was happy to leave Syl's woods without running into anyone else. It was adventure enough to try to puzzle out the hiking trails at Red River Gorge. There were a lot of arches to visit. Silvermine Arch, with its rickety wooden steps down to a pool at the mouth of a cave, was supposed to be near John Swift's silver mine of the 1760s. Moonshiner's Arch, with its natural chimney hole for a smoking still, recalls one of the few ways to earn cash in a culture rich in many ways other than economic. It's said that some of the modest brick houses around the gorge were built by Prohibition money. Music is another legacy of the gorge: Lily May Ledford, the banjo-playing leader of the first women's string band at the Grand Ole Opry, grew up picking berries at Chimney Top. Once, in a sheltered little cove, I stumbled onto a cemetery and found a headstone with a poem full of love for Dog Holler.

In the 1970s, the Army Corps of Engineers tried to dam the gorge, but fierce local opposition helped stop them. The controversy attracted many new visitors. A lot of arches are only a few miles off a road, resulting in trail networks that are far more chaotic than shown on the map. I just wanted a nice place to picnic, where I could savor Syl's conserve and let ginseng and the gorge work their will on me. But I found myself turning irresolutely from map to reality and back again. Which one would take me to the right spot, and which was likely to get me, as they say in Utah, rimrocked? It may have been the opposite of Daniel Boone's trailless terrain, but it still was plumb bewildering.

# FIVE

# SIZE IS AS SIZE DOES

"I'VE GOT TO GO SOAK MY HEAD," MARCIA BONTA SAID.

I didn't blame her. Not yet nine in the morning, but already the air was desperately muggy. This would prove to be the hottest July in many years in south-central Pennsylvania, the kind of weather that truly makes you sweat over global warming. But Marcia was grinning. One of the most congenial people I've ever met, and by far the friendliest writer, Marcia was always jolly, even when she was miserable. She cheerfully completed the last check of all the tents, tables, and porta-potties set up in her yard. She and her husband, Bruce, were hosting a statewide annual meeting of the Pennsylvania Forest Stewardship Program.

It took a lot of planning to host a workshop for 140 people, but Marcia and Bruce were good at planning. Today they would demonstrate what they planned for the future of their 640 acres—one square mile of forest. They had gone to considerable trouble and expense to compose an official forest plan that formalized doing nothing.

Marcia's high cheekbones and wide-set eyes were crowned by a head of luxuriant gray hair. She usually wore it pulled back from her face, which was typically lit with a smile. She grew up in southern New Jersey but learned to love Pennsylvania from her father, who took her hiking in the mountains where he had grown up. She was a born naturalist but went to college to become an English teacher because science wasn't a serious option for a girl in the 1950s. At college, she met Bruce, and they moved here to Plummer's Hollow thirty years ago when Bruce took a job as a librarian at Penn State. Entranced by her surroundings, and determined to stay home to raise her three sons, Marcia began to write.

Her articles on natural history for various magazines eventually accumulated into the hundreds. Her first book, *Escape to the Mountain,* in 1980, described the early struggles of getting settled at Plummer's Hollow in a genteel old house well on its way to ramshackle. Reading her prose, you can feel the intense curiosity that drove Marcia to make a lifestyle of solitary, hours-long walks every day to learn what the wild was doing. Over the years, her family and friends built eleven miles of trail for her, with benches. Her day-by-day series of notes on the seasons, *Appalachian Spring, Appalachian Summer,* and *Appalachian Autumn* (with *Appalachian Winter* under way), brought her widespread acclaim. I learned about her through those books. By the time I got to Plummer's Hollow, I already knew some of its secrets.

The hollow rises above the Little Juniata River. Across the bridge and beyond the railroad tracks there is a gate, and inside the gate is a wooden box with handouts and a hikers' sign-in book. "Welcome to the Plummer's Hollow Private Nature Reserve," states an eighteen-page trail guide. "We hope you will enjoy the birds, animals, plants, and peace, and we trust that you will not disturb anything during your walk." The long, straight driveway runs for more than a mile along a splashing creek and through a deep, shady hemlock forest. The trail guide describes seventeen stops along the way. Included are stumps of two large pine trees believed cut around 1813, the remnants of a hearth where charcoal was made to fuel a nearby iron forge in operation around that time, and stone blocks from a cistern built in 1850 to supply water to the steam locomotives on the line between Philadelphia and Pittsburgh.

The man in charge of the cistern, William Plummer, bought fifty-five acres near the top of the hollow, built the house, and established a farm and apple orchard. For a century thereafter, the

Plummer family purchased, swapped, and sold additional tracts, cutting timber now and again as financial vicissitudes dictated, until no more Plummers were left in the area. The Bontas began with 162 acres of former Plummer land and added to it as surrounding pieces became available for sale—or, rather, as they began to be logged.

Some of Marcia's favorite places on the ridges bordering Plummer's Hollow were clear-cut despite years of negotiations to save them. Absentee owners, foresters, and lumbermen reneged on promises, lied outright, and vandalized the gate repeatedly. Then they razed the mountainside, which threatened to cover the Bontas' driveway with landslides. Watching the bulldozers work made Marcia sleepless and prone to nightmares when she finally did drift off. Her walks became circumscribed as she avoided denuded places where earlier she had observed coyotes, black bears, foxes, ruffed grouse, and innumerable smaller creatures.

When she and Bruce were able to buy other tracts of surrounding land, they were determined to protect what they owned from a similar fate. They wanted the natural processes that Marcia monitored with patient, loving, and scientifically informed observations to continue indefinitely without human disturbance. They used a federal-state program called Forest Stewardship to compose a forest management plan that said exactly that.

The Forest Stewardship Program that helped the Bontas draw up their plan is one of dozens offered by both state and federal agencies, sometimes for free, sometimes on a cost-share basis. The easiest entrance into the bureaucratic maze is to look in the phone book or on the Internet for the local representative of the state forestry department or extension service. There are programs for professional assistance in everything from clear-cutting to wildlife habitat enhancement. It doesn't take a cynic to notice that many services are heavily tilted toward industrial production of wood.

But that doesn't diminish the value of planning. Planning has been an essential component of good forestry since at least the nineteenth century. Early on, it became obvious that the most fundamental task of forestry must be to regulate the harvest according to growth. The principle of "sustained yield" became the guiding science of silviculture. It was based on the sensible proposition that only as much timber should be harvested as the forest could grow over a unit of time, usually a decade. Foresters developed indices of growth rates for individual tree species and measures of productivity for individual sites to establish amounts that could be harvested without diminishing future supplies. Broadening that original notion toward true sustainability merely requires enlarging the scope from timber to everything we take from the forest.

To know how much you can take from the forest, you need to know how much there is, so inventories, maps, and detailed descriptions of the land are essential. Surely one of the basic obligations of ownership is to know something about what you own. To get some sense, however narrowed by tunnel vision or colored by culture, of how a piece of ecosystem functions, it's worth finding a forester from a public or private service to gather the data and write a report. By then applying the data gained from an analysis of the land, landowner demands (or, as foresters diplomatically call them, landowner desires) can be shaped by ecosystem limits. Planning offers a process to move from egocentric to ecocentric uses of the land.

Learning about their land is important to many woodlot owners. That's why more than a hundred of them were milling around tables of brochures and handouts in Marcia's yard, at the edge of a large field. Two common yellowthroats sang *wichity-wichity-wichity* to each other across the meadow while people mingled around the coolers and gratefully sipped cold drinks. The workshop focused on biodiversity and the impact of various human activities on it. Differences in philosophies crystallized in Bruce's description of a blowdown from a small tornado that had passed through one spring. In *Appalachian Autumn,* Marcia noted that "by late summer, winter wrens could be seen flitting through the underbrush beneath the fallen trees. . . . [Their] cavelike nests are hollowed into the earth of uprooted trees, under the bark, or beneath stream banks."

A forester in the audience suggested that selectively salvaging the downed trees might not cause any loss to the ecosystem. But would the winter wrens have chosen it had the blowdown been less tangled? Rather than take a chance, or act in the absence of knowledge, the Bontas preferred to allow the forest its own self-willed succession, without human intervention. No intervention, that is, with one pesky exception: deer.

The only active management the Bontas do (besides maintaining two old fields and the forest trails) is to allow hunting. They were driven to it by Marcia's close attention, over decades, to the state of the flora around her. She saw that several species of plants were disappearing due to deer browsing. Pennsylvania's troubles with overabundant deer herds are legendary. A disharmonic convergence of time and circumstances, involving the extirpation of predators, the protection of deer after nineteenth-century market-hunting extravaganzas, and the browse produced by extensive timbering, caused chronic deer irruptions throughout much of the twentieth century. Many other states had similar conditions and experienced similar results, but Pennsylvania was one of the worst examples.

When deer reach populations greater than about twenty per square mile, they radically change the forest. They browse some six hundred species of plants, including many endangered or threatened ones. Seedlings of their favorite canopy and understory species, such as oaks, hemlocks, sugar maple, viburnums, and greenbrier, are browsed into oblivion. As these plants fail to regenerate, the composition of the forest shifts, sometimes even turning into savanna. Dozens of bird species nest or forage within six feet of the forest floor, and when the plants they depend on disappear, so do the birds.

Some years earlier, Marcia and Bruce had built a small, fenced deer exclosure in their woods, just to see what might come up. Immediately, Solomon's seal and Canada mayflowers, which had largely disappeared elsewhere on the property, began to grow. A biologist friend who was a deer expert recommended that thirty to forty deer be harvested from their land each year. Bruce wasn't a hunter, but when he and Marcia moved in, they had not posted their land, in keeping with community traditions. Gradually, though, they had more and more hunter troubles. The boys' pet dog was shot not far from the house. Marcia counted a dozen hunters from her kitchen window one fall despite large safety-zone signs. And still the deer proliferated.

So they changed their strategy. They limited hunting to those with written permission only, and gave that permission—and keys to their gate—to about twenty hunters they selected after talking to their neighbors and others in the community. Many of these hunters come from families that have hunted the area for generations but owned no land themselves. The Bontas welcome friends and family members of the hunters as well, as long as the hunters are willing to take responsibility for them. Turkey as well as deer can be hunted. One Sunday afternoon every September, the Bontas hold a meeting for all the hunters. Bruce gives out copies of a map of the property and asks that each hunter mark where and what he or she kills so that the harvest can be monitored. Any concerns of the Bontas or the hunters are discussed frankly and in depth.

The new system not only has strengthened the Bontas' relationship with the community, but also is visibly reducing the impact of deer on the land. Plus, it supplies the Bontas with plenty of venison and yard-long deer bolognas. In the most recent season, the hunters killed forty-four deer, after several years of averaging around thirty. The hunters also act as property patrols and send strangers packing. They work on trail maintenance. And they help with such things as parking, registration, and trail guiding when the Bontas host a forest workshop.

After this latest workshop ended, the Bontas and several of their hunter friends sat, exhausted, around the white-pillared porch of the old house. Talk about the presentations turned inexorably to stories about the land. A man named Troy began by saying ruefully that no one would believe him, but he wanted to share an experience he'd had while turkey hunting during spring gobbler season. Camouflaged and discreet, as turkey hunters must be, he was sitting near the point above Plummer's Hollow that he likes best, listening and calling. Suddenly, from somewhere above him in the oak against which he leaned, Troy heard a voice exclaim, "You can't hide!" He looked up to see a crow landing on a branch. "You can't hide!" the crow cried again, looking directly at him. Troy grabbed his rifle and ran out of there. Marcia listened carefully. Crows fall out of nests, and people sometimes raise them. Like every other wild creature, crows have capacities far beyond our ken. The group on the veranda puzzled over possible explanations, trying to keep an open mind, knowing that lessons from nature come in complex forms. The Bontas' plan is to keep the lessons coming, even if no one can quite figure out what they mean.

---

"When Good Plans Go Bad" could be the headline for the Robbins family's experience in Rutherford County, North Carolina. Their story is one of sustainability looking for a place to happen but stymied, not only by the allied forces of industrial capitalism, but also by a neighbor's rage.

Dusk was falling as I pulled into the yard of the old Hemphill house, and steam was rising off a large pan in an open shed. A deliciously sugary smell wafted on the breeze. It was late September, and Donna and Rodney Robbins were making sorghum molasses with Donna's parents, Mr. and Mrs. Hemphill. Their people had been doing this for at least five generations. The clapboard house beyond the shed was built in 1900 from boards sawn by Donna's great-grandfather. In a corner cupboard in the living room, a little wood placard was painted with the homily that could serve as the Appalachian national anthem:

> Use it up
> Wear it out
> Make it do
> Or do without

It was advice passed on by earlier Hemphills, who were among the first families to settle on Cove Creek. One of Donna's great-great-grandmothers, at two and a half years old, was scalped and lived, but her hair never grew back, and she always wore a bonnet. Later, the family legend goes, Indians would go out of their way while traveling to pay reverent attention to her. By 1846, John and Louisa Hemphill had purchased four hundred acres on both sides of Cove Creek for $1,900. John was a farmer and postmaster, Louisa a weaver who made flax and woolen blankets. She owned the first sewing machine in the cove. They also owned slaves. Two of their three sons were killed in the Civil War.

"Israel Leander had cleared off a field in preparation for building a house and getting married," Donna said, "but he never came back from the war. We still call it the Lee Field, even though it's long since grown back into trees."

The Hemphills had a vested interest in keeping their land productive for the future. That nine-year-old vested interest was named James, and just then he was chewing on a cane of sorghum. Sorghum refers to a genus of cornlike grasses native to Africa and Asia and cultivated since ancient times for grain and syrup. A heap of long, skinny canes extended over the tailgate of Uncle Wade's pickup truck, which was backed up to the press. A permanent fixture in the yard, the press was a big, rusty device of rollers and cogs, turned by a wide, black belt running around a large flywheel and a smaller flywheel on a tractor nearby. The belts formerly were powered by horses turning in a circle, and the press was moved from one cane patch to another to serve many families.

Donna worked as a school librarian; her husband, Rodney, farmed the four hundred acres that belonged to her father and three hundred more that he leased. Rodney first met Donna as a teenager when he went tubing down Cove Creek with very rowdy friends. Donna's father came down and warned them off his property, even pulling a pistol when the boys talked back. Rodney noticed the redhead standing behind her father. A few years later, they began to date, and he fell in love with the sparkly personality that matched her hair.

Rodney was broad-shouldered and narrow-hipped, with dark eyebrows and a neatly trimmed beard flecked with gray. His smile could brighten a dim room. His grandfather logged with mules, and his great-uncle owned a sawmill. After Rodney started farming with Donna's father, he noticed woodlands with decent timber. Now half of his annual income comes from working the woods in winter, including running his own mill. The other half comes from summer crops of corn, soybeans, and hay.

I had toured the farm's woodlands with Rodney earlier that day. The landscape of Appalachian foothills was dusty with autumn but still sticky with summer. The woods had been logged around 1950 to buy out Donna's father's siblings, but not everything was clear-cut. The trees were mostly young, but already a diverse understory was developing. Pines were thick in some places; in others, they mixed with plenty of hardwoods. Rodney preferred to practice selection harvesting, choosing individual trees according to maturity and condition, and leaving the best trees to grow better. When ice storms and southern pine beetles devastated some of his pine stands, he spent years salvaging the best of the lumber. He planted ginseng and walnut trees. He was thinking twenty-five to fifty years ahead. This was the kind of approach he wanted his land-use plan to reflect.

In North Carolina, landowners must have a land-use plan to qualify for the land-use taxation rate. Taxes can be the most burdensome landowner responsibility, especially when they are artificially driven upward by sprawl development. Land-use taxation, usually based on the productivity of the soil, helps mitigate this effect and can considerably reduce the tax burden for farmers. On a tight farm budget like the Robbinses', it's a necessity. When Rodney contacted the North Carolina Department of Forestry to obtain the required plan, he said he wanted it based on selection harvesting. Instead, his plan directed him to clear-cut and plant loblolly pine, the darling tree of industry because of its quick growth and ease of processing.

"Seems like the foresters are tied in with industry," Rodney said, "and getting the landowners to feed into it, too."

The conversion of natural forests to monocultural plantations is one of the great issues of contemporary forestry. "Plantation" has varied meanings; in its fullest sense, it refers to artificially planted, fertilized, and intensively managed trees of a single, often non-native species. Growing wood as an agricultural crop in this way can produce ten times more fiber per acre than natural forest, plus it's more uniform for the mill and often of better quality for pulp. Rotations can be as short as seven years. Trees that have been genetically engineered to grow even faster and produce their own herbicide will soon contribute to plantation efficiency—as well as to problems like toxic pollen drift, already being demonstrated by other genetically modified crops. Plantations are typically able to sustain only very small portions of the former biodiversity of natural forest.

It's difficult to determine the amount of land in plantations, because statistics usually give only general timberland acreage. On a global level, the best estimate at the end of the twentieth century was one-third of a billion acres, or about 3 percent of total world forest. Industry analysts forecast a much more expansive role for plantations as world demand for wood grows. Most plantations have been established since 1950, and three-quarters of all plantation acreage grows conifers in temperate regions, with the largest single chunk (about one-fifth of the total) in the former Soviet Union.

China has nearly that much and is said to be furiously afforesting, which means planting trees on land that does not currently grow forest. Reforesting means the planting of trees on existing forested land that has been timbered. By afforesting with plantations, China hopes to reduce the pressure on its few remaining natural forests. Only in situations like this, when plantations do not arise from the conversion of existing natural forests, can they contribute to sustainability. Established on degraded former agricultural soils, as they increasingly are in Brazil and other tropical countries, such plantations may be an ecologically as well as economically valid choice, especially if native tree species are planted. After all, even the shortest tree rotations are longer than an annual crop, and even the most simplified forest can support more biodiversity than a field of corn.

On the other hand, plantations fail to offer a benefit once widely touted by industry: the sequestration of more carbon than natural forests. Carbon dioxide is the gas that drives global warming by trapping the sun's heat inside the earth's atmosphere. The burning of fossil fuels gives off huge quantities. Trees absorb carbon as they grow and store it in wood, a fact that makes forests crucial to the world carbon budget. For years, the wood industry argued that young, rapidly growing trees acted as carbon sinks, sucking more out of the atmosphere than old, slow-growing trees possibly could.

The international attempt to reduce global carbon dioxide emissions, the Kyoto Protocol, was not even signed by the country responsible for a quarter of all emissions—namely, the United States. But it did spur research efforts into the biogeochemical nature of carbon flow. Studies began to find that the original calculations were much too limited. Carbon dioxide is released back to the atmosphere at whatever point the wood decays, whether in a forest or as boards or paper in a landfill, so the entire life cycle of all the harvested wood has to be figured in. So does the entire life cycle of a forest. The older a forest grows without disturbance, the more time it has to fix carbon both in wood and in the soil. It turns out that disruption of the soil by cutting mature forests to replace them with young, more frequently harvested trees could dramatically increase atmospheric carbon.

But by now the momentum of tree plantations is well established in the Southeast. Following the bruising timber wars in the Pacific Northwest, corporate interest shifted. There was much less protected federal land in the Southeast, and state regulations were looser. More than half of all commercial plantations in the United States are now located in the South, from Virginia to Texas, and pulpwood production has been increasing every year for two decades. Twenty percent of the southeastern forested landscape is owned by the wood products industry, more than in any other section of the country. Industry influence extends beyond those borders through the hunger of huge mills, especially chip mills.

A hundred and fifty new chip mills were built in the Southeast in the 1990s alone, consuming more than a million acres of trees a year. A century after the first round of industrial timbering deforested large parts of Appalachia, many Appalachian states approached or surpassed historic levels of timber harvest. Pines are now being harvested faster than they grow, a cardinal infraction of sustained yield. Hardwood cutting is accelerating toward that same point. Clear-cuts are large and abundant throughout the region.

Chip mills seem designed not only for high yields from industry pine plantations, but also for the conversion of established and maturing hardwood forests like Rodney's. The year before, Rodney had been nudged hard toward industrial production by the arrival of Willamette's new chip mill in Union Mills. I was going to visit it tomorrow.

Rodney had already explained the politics connecting the local sawmill family to the new mill. He hoped that the chip mill would provide a market for his low-value logs, which would advance his own interests as well as the mill's. But so far, he was finding that situation to be elusive, because mill policy was geared to support the biggest suppliers. Whenever there was a downturn in the volatile wood products market, the mill would buy logs only from them.

Driven by the local tax assessor, who administered the land-use tax, Rodney had ended up making several clear-cuts of six to seven acres in order to qualify. He was frustrated and angry. When he saw a notice in the newspaper about a meeting on sustainable forestry by Concerned Citizens of Rutherford County, a group formed to protest the new chip mill, he said to Donna, "That looks like what I want." He attended workshops and started fencing the woods when he learned that cattle would hurt his tree regeneration. Finally, after trying to work with the tax assessor and state foresters to change the forest stewardship plan, Rodney and Donna wrote their own, complete with a glossary of definitions and citations from scientific papers.

Rodney turned it in to the county assessor a year ago and hadn't heard since. He took this as tacit acceptance of the plan. And by now he had other things to worry about.

Clearly a mechanical genius, Rodney made a hobby out of going to auctions to pick up bargains on used equipment. He bought a skidder for $1,600, fixed the gears, and rebuilt the motor. He also had a couple of small knuckleboom loaders. His greatest achievement, though, was the sawmill. It was a double ought Frick of 1950s vintage that he bought for $1,000 about fifteen years ago. He replaced the wooden rails with steel and repaired various other parts. With it, he milled his own trees, mostly, although he cut some locust posts for a friend who needed fencing. He sold his boards to local mills. He could saw four thousand board feet a day of good logs and earn $300 per thousand board feet for the milled lumber. He would have been paid only $230 per thousand board feet for twelve-inch-diameter logs and larger. Smaller logs brought even less, so milling and selling his own small logs gave Rodney a small but important economic advantage.

"Poplar is the money tree," he said. "I sawed two trees up and sold the boards for fifteen-hundred dollars." He also mills short-leaf and Virginia pines.

Or he did, until last month. We stood by the deeply charred posts that had held up a metal roof over the mill. The power unit had been torched by an arsonist. Rodney had considered insurance but had figured he would probably save enough on the premiums to take care of anything short of catastrophe. He knows who did it. A neighbor, a young man, was driving a pickup through one of Rodney's fields, tearing it up. Rodney told him to leave. Feuds are not unknown here; Donna's maternal grandmother sewed a special pocket in the front of her husband's overalls for a pistol to protect himself against neighbors who had something against him. Her paternal grandfather had been deputy sheriff and had enemies who turned over his sorghum molasses barrels, wasting all that work.

Donna was unpacking quart glass jars to catch the finished molasses when she told me this. "What do you do?" she asked. "You don't want to lie down and be walked on, but you don't want to escalate it either." She went over to talk with the young man's father. "I asked him what we had done to get such retaliation, and he listed all kinds of crazy things that he said were all Rodney's fault."

"If I didn't believe in hell," Rodney said, "I'd be thinking about revenge."

But at least for that night, the bitterness of loss dissolved in the sweetness of cooking sorghum. Leaves had been stripped off the load of canes in the back of the pickup by Donna's uncle Wade, whose cane they were making on shares. Each share would include molasses from the beginning, middle, and end of the run, so they would all get the full spectrum. There's a lot of variation in molasses; men made reputations on their skill with sorghum.

Mrs. Hemphill, Donna's mother, remembered when everybody would get together to make molasses and the children stripped the leaves. Her father used molasses as one of their main money crops. Her brother Wade planned to sell some of his quarts.

"Cane's not as tall as when I was a boy," Wade said. "It used to be fourteen foot; now it's eight to ten."

I had seen gullies higher than my head elsewhere in the county, so I was acquainted with the legacy of soil erosion from the days when cotton was raised in the area. But the long switches of canes were impressive enough as Wade fed sheaves of them from the tailgate of his pickup into the rollers of the press. He pitchforked the limp, spent stalks into mounds below the press and would later feed them to his cattle.

From the rollers poured a milky, green juice that frothed as it streamed into a muslin-covered barrel below the press. The barrel emptied through an underground hose across the yard to another muslin-covered barrel at the edge of the open shed. Then the juice slid into the large, rectangular, copper-sheathed and baffled cooking pan. A fire crackled underneath.

Mr. and Mrs. Hemphill did the serious molasses making. Theirs was a dance choreographed by fifty years of experience. He stoked the fire beneath the pan, skimmed the green froth off the molasses, raked the thin fluid into baffle after baffle to reduce but not scorch it, then stoked the fire again. The final stream that poured from the downside corner of the pan was thick as taffy but more gracile, stretching like a cat whenever the air from our passage moved it. Mrs. Hemphill filtered and bottled it while she watched Mr. Hemphill, knowing just what he'd need next and getting it for him, and he skimmed and raked and fired, knowing that she knew. They gave me a heavy quart of what looked like smoked honey. I plunged a spoon into it as soon as I got home. Flavors of butterscotch and amber melted in my mouth, the taste of a golden autumn.

———————

Steam rose from a thirty-foot mound of wood chips in the first warming rays of morning sun. A few days ago, the chips were trees growing across the landscape somewhere within a hundred miles of Union Mills, North Carolina. Here, at the mill that Willamette built, logs are debarked, chipped into fragments, graded, and loaded onto train cars and trucks to be transported to some other mill. There they are recombined in industrial slurries to produce mountains of paper and mammoth rolls of cardboard packaging. Pulp is the ultimate fate of most chips, although increasing amounts are used for composite boards, which are the timber industry's response to shrinking wood supplies and increasing demands. With a production capacity of three hundred thousand tons of chips a year, Willamette's mill in Union Mills is a typical example of the chip mill phenomenon, complete with protesters.

Willamette Industries began as a lumber company in Oregon in 1906 and is still headquartered in Portland. But today Willamette is diversified in both geography and production, with 105 plants in twenty-four states, Europe, and Mexico, and some fourteen thousand employees. It owns 1.7 million acres of timberlands, mostly in Oregon and Louisiana, which produce about two-thirds of the wood necessary to feed its mills. Willamette has net annual sales of some $4 billion annually on brown and white papers, corrugated containers, plywood, and various composite boards. Some of its paper mills are located in Kentucky and Tennessee. "Those are expanding," said Shannon Buckley, Willamette's procurement forester and the only Willamette employee at Union Mills. "So we need dependable sources of chips." The mill's six other permanent full-time workers are employees of the locally based Broad River Company, which leases and operates it.

I met Shannon at the scale house at the mill's entrance. He was very tall and thin, blue-eyed and sandy-haired under the required helmet, and spoke with a southern drawl he'd picked up from two decades of living in the area. He had been described by members of the Concerned Citizens of Rutherford County, the local group that had organized to combat the mill, as a gentleman.

Patient and courteous, Shannon explained how the mill bought pulpwood by the ton, weighing the log trucks before they were unloaded by the huge crane and again afterward. We climbed the steel tower to the crane's control room, where a man wielding two joysticks watched what he was doing on a TV monitor. We made what were probably the usual video game jokes.

"You missed a log," the crane operator was informed by the truck driver below on the radio.

"That sun angle makes a bad glare," Shannon told him. "Get whatever shade you need."

Next, the logs went into the debarker, a twelve-foot-tall, ninety-foot-long drum where they are bounced together, knocking the bark off. Fortunately for my decibel tolerance, the mill was shut down because of a temporary delay in the arrival of the CSX Railroad cars to carry off the chips. In the empty debarker control room, there was a boom box, photos of children, and a satisfyingly large, red button marked "Emergency Stop."

"It amounts to twenty-plus tractor-trailer loads of bark a week," Shannon said. "We sell it for use as mulch on playgrounds and walkways."

Outside again, we watched bluebirds land on the motionless debarker conveyor belts, picking up reddish strands that spilled every which way. The mill took up twenty-five acres near the middle of a two-hundred-acre former dairy farm, which Shannon made sure was a model of thoughtful management. The annual company picnic is held on the shore of the pond. I could see a hunter's deer stand in a tree at the edge of the woods.

"We sited the buildings to have as much buffer from neighbors as possible," Shannon said. "The amount of trucks on the road is the biggest change for the local residents." Residents do, in fact, complain bitterly about, among other things, the heavy, dangerous trucks and the degenerating railroad crossing.

A Carolina wren sang somewhere as we entered the mill's chipping chamber, where we passed a man sharpening some of the chipping knives. This must be done several times daily. The mill only took hardwoods at this point, Shannon said. "If we eventually go to the softer pines, our two hundred-horsepower knife blades would be more than adequate."

The mill ran only one shift, 7 A.M. to 5 P.M. "Loggers don't work at night," Shannon said. Once shredded, the chips are screened, with large ones thrown back in and fine ones sifted out and sold for boiler fuel to a textile and a pharmaceutical plant. Conveyor belts take the chips to a railroad tipple, where electronic eyes sense movement and activate a winch to pull each railcar forward.

"It's a very simple system," Shannon said. "The mill is designed to operate this way, without major equipment overhaul, for twenty to twenty-five years."

He explained the basic rules for loggers. "We accept three- to twenty-two-inch-diameter trees, with knots trimmed off. It has to be sound wood, not decayed or charred. Crooked is OK; the trees don't have to be pretty. We do ask loggers to cut and load the least crooked way. A Willamette officer made a slip of the tongue by saying we would take stumps; that's not true, we do not. We don't buy cedar; if we catch it, we'll load it back. Loggers know exactly how to hide things in their loads, the way they pack the logs. It's our prerogative to turn down a whole load if some are undersize, but we try to show them why it's a problem.

"Loggers have to notify me ahead of time about insurance, worker's comp, and the liability coverages required by law. If the law doesn't require it, I do exclude some part-time and small-scale loggers from our requirements, or I'll try to get another company to cover them under its name. This year we'll buy three and a half to four million dollars' worth of pulpwood from about a hundred twenty different logging contractors, most of whom have crews of three to four people. When there's a market downturn and I have to restrict input, I go by proportion and give our biggest suppliers the biggest quotas."

I mentioned certification, and Shannon grimaced. "I dread it," he said. "We don't track the exact location or type of harvest our wood comes from. Ninety-five percent of it is clear-cut, I'm guessing. The Forest Stewardship Council requirements don't fit industrial forestry. Willamette supports educational efforts, we work with state foresters, we probably will soon require that our loggers have training. Most of them have had it already. We've also pushed for the state to fund more water-quality foresters, but that hasn't happened so far."

Outside the mill, we stopped once again at the pile of logs—roughly eight thousand trees—that encircled the now-motionless crane. "Some of the wood we get would appear to be good sawtimber," Shannon said, touching on one of the major objections raised by his opponents, "but there's no market for it. Like hickory—furniture people don't like it. Furniture people pay a high price for clear lumber, but for the less desirable, they pay less. So loggers may get more at the chip mill. Most of the trees that come in are older trees; a lot of them are hollow. We don't have a whole lot that a sawmill wants—a little, there's always a little overlap."

I noticed a group of large, debarked trees off to the side. Some were hollow; one in particular was very thick in girth but mostly air. They were rejects, too large for the chipper. It was painful to see these great wildlife den trees wasted. Chip mill employees cut some up for firewood.

"We're going to start splitting them," Shannon said, "so then we can chip them."

Willamette spent five years navigating the economic, environmental, legal, and social factors involved in building this mill. Still, it couldn't avoid controversy, especially given its history of EPA violations. The local group, Concerned Citizens of Rutherford County, joined the Dogwood Alliance, a nonprofit regional coalition of more than seventy grassroots and community organizations. The goal of the Dogwood Alliance is to stop the expansion of chip mills and the accompanying industrial style of forestry. Staff compile data on over-cutting, clear-cutting, and associated environmental damage and mobilize widespread opposition. The alliance challenges major paper suppliers such as Staples and lumber retailers such as Lowe's and Home Depot to reject wood products made from public lands or old growth anywhere. In its own, postconsumer recycled publications, the alliance urges everyone to rethink the whole process of supply and demand by which Americans, who constitute 6 percent of the world's population, consume 30 percent of the entire world output of wood products.

But it wasn't Dogwood people that locked down at Broad River Mill one fine spring morning in May 1999. It was Katuah Earth First!, the southern Appalachian cell of the legendary organization of anarchists for the environment. Anarchy is for the young, and Earth First!ers tend to be young and passionate, in the manner of student revolutionaries in tzarist Russia, with wild and crazy hair and wire-rimmed glasses. Four Earth First!ers hung all day from the crane, while several dozen others below carried out supportive demonstrations. Shannon had video footage of it in his office back at the scale house.

I was interested in seeing the tape, because I knew what led up to the action. Forty-five people had trained intensively for months, synchronizing every detail. At 3:30 A.M. on the chosen day, the crew with the banner set out for their target. At 4:30 A.M., the first lock-down group set out, carrying chains bolted on their wrists and other necessary paraphernalia. Other activists followed at timed intervals, including some that delivered press releases to a spectrum of media outlets. The point was to wrest the public's attention away from the usual multitudinous other distractions and stimulate discussion of how society makes and uses paper. It promised to be the largest, best-planned action ever in western North Carolina.

At approximately 5 A.M., in the moonless predawn dark, the first six lock-downers were driving a sport utility vehicle (borrowed from the driver's mother) at exactly the speed limit around a curve. A possum stepped into the road. The driver swerved, so did the possum, and the SUV fishtailed at fifty-five miles an hour and then flipped three times down the middle of the road until it came to rest upright. The only person not wearing a seat belt was ejected out the back window into the pitch blackness. The SUV was a total loss, its roof buckled in, its windows crumbled. The possum went on about his business.

Slowly, groaning with pain from broken bones and multiple cuts, the five remaining in the vehicle got out and discovered that one was missing. Four of them began feeling through the dark for a body, and one flagged down the next passing car and asked the terrified lady driver to take him back down the road.

A few miles farther, another group of lock-downers was waiting at a staging area. A strange car pulled up, and an Earth First!er rolled out onto the pavement. "He needs help," a female voice gasped, and she sped off. The man was dazed and stumbling and covered with blood. "Call 911," he managed to say. "And call off the action, there's been a wreck."

The Earth First! medical crew took off for the crash site. With feverish haste but determined calm, the remaining lock-downers pulled together. They intercepted arriving activists. They recalled the banner crew. They sent the press release distributors rushing back to their dropoff points. Someone gathered the equipment and stashed it out of sight. Someone else hid the truckload of stumps. Thirty-nine people in full mission operation were located and their activities reversed. Then they all carpooled to the hospital, where the ragtag band filled the waiting room. Under the curious stares of early shift nurses, they wept with relief that there was no loss of life and congratulated themselves on a highly successful mission abortion. As the injured members recuperated, the group bonded even more strongly and felt tempered by a dry run full of adversity.

Shannon heard about the aborted raid the next day. "Someone who monitors an environmental listserv told us about it," he said. "There was talk about several people being in the hospital." Shannon had anticipated protests from the start and had discussed the possibilities with the sheriff. When the real action came a few months later, it was handled fairly calmly, with ten arrests over a period of six hours. Five protesters chained their arms together in steel pipes placed through hollowed-out stumps. The sheriff had to take each 300-pound stump and pipe combination apart with a lifesaving tool called the jaws of life to extricate the five for arrest. Someone beat on a drum as a larger group chanted, "Shut down Willamette! Save our planet!" A speaker with a microphone described how "Willamette destroys our jobs, forests, and rivers." Four protesters hung in harnesses from the crane, two of them holding an Earth First! banner made from second-hand sheets.

"After six hours of twisting around in the wind, one girl wasn't feeling too well; she was sunburned and throwing up," Shannon said. "The demonstration didn't hurt us per se. There was no property damage. We couldn't move chips because people were hanging on the crane, but that's not a big deal. I don't expect them back, because they know the media will only cover the same issue so many times."

The receptionist, a pretty, dark-haired young woman, came in to watch a few minutes of the tape with us. "Their signs are made of cardboard," she pointed out.

---

Shopping, but not in a mall! Local artisans! Local materials! Berea, Kentucky, on the western edge of the Cumberland Plateau, seems a good place for moral instruction on the insidious nature of consumerism. Founded on a Christian ethic of right living, the town was established in 1853 by noted Kentucky abolitionist Cassius M. Clay and his friend the Reverend John G. Fee. Their goal was a form of sustainability suited to the times: a community that would demonstrate the advantages of free labor over slavery. The name was chosen for a biblical town where the people "received the Word with all readiness of mind." In 1855, Fee established the multiracial, coeducational, tuition-free, nondenominational liberal arts school that would become Berea College.

Such radical social innovations in a proslavery area drew hostile attention from other communities, which forced the school to close and its leaders to flee until after the Civil War. They returned to recruit freed slaves and educate them into careers and an integrated community, until in 1904 a state law aimed at Berea made interracial education illegal. College lawyers appealed the law to the U.S. Supreme Court, which ruled against them. Forced to segregate, college president William G. Frost led a drive to raise money for a separate African-American school, Lincoln Institute, near Louisville. He expanded Berea's long-established commitment to poor Appalachian whites and realized their potential contribution to the crafts revival under way nationally at the time. And he hired Silas C. Mason to be the first college forester.

The result today is a highly ranked academic institution of fifteen hundred students embedded in a town of about ten thousand people, most of whom are concerned in one way or another with preserving Appalachian heritage. Berea is the acknowledged folk arts and crafts capital of Kentucky. Several colorful clusters of art, craft, gift, and antique shops, interspersed with places to eat, are located in Old Town around Berea College, which offers free walking tours through a tree-studded campus several times daily during the summer season. There could hardly be a lovelier place to go shopping. Beyond the town lie eight thousand acres of college forestland and, through the far-sighted vision of Mason, town watershed.

Berea College is a relatively small example of the category of institutional forest owners. Associations of all kinds, from old-fashioned hunting clubs to newly emerging aggregates of forest investors called

TIMOs (timber investment management organizations), often control larger acreages. None, however, has the historic drive toward sustainability that characterizes Berea. From its inception, the college admitted only students with high ability but limited finances. Each student earns room and board through the college work program and receives a full tuition scholarship from private college endowments. To keep maintenance expenses to a minimum and create a culture of service, it has always been in the college's best interests to develop a sustainable community.

The shops are full of beautiful things: baskets, quilts, weavings, pottery, brass, iron, candles, toys, paintings, sculptures, prints, photographs, musical instruments, and above all, fine wood furniture. I ran reverent fingers across the polished surfaces of oak tables and the smooth rungs of maple chairs, examples of a perfect union between materials and method. Most of the wood comes from local landscapes through informal networks of small-scale artisans and suppliers.

Scales of consumption drive scales of impact on the earth. Environmental degradation is not a simple corollary of population growth, as is usually presented in the media. Because Americans consume more of everything than anyone else, each individual American is responsible for more environmental destruction than any Third World family, no matter how many children the parents have. And every new American, whether native born or immigrant, arrives with expectations to attain our present level of materialism. Clearly, it's not the other peoples of the world who need to stop increasing, but us Americans.

This perspective on the issue of world population growth is not widely shared in this country, although it's nearly global beyond it. Given our current patterns of consumption, our lifestyles are physically unsustainable for the long-term future, either for the few if they manage to fend off the many, or for the many if the next new world order somehow becomes egalitarian. Either way, the destruction caused by consumption must be reduced.

Besides total collapse into chaos, there are several options. We could voluntarily shrink our lifestyles dramatically, in a selfless sacrifice to the best interests of the planet. This seems unlikely. Or we could adopt national policies aimed at stabilizing population growth instead of subsidizing it. Ideological wars would be sure to follow.

A more pragmatic course of action is laid out by the Global Green Deal. In his book, *Earth Odyssey: Around the World in Search of Our Environmental Future,* author Mark Hertsgaard formulates a plan to make repairing the planet's ravaged environment the biggest jobs-and-business program ever. Inspired by President Franklin Roosevelt's New Deal in the Depression of the 1930s, Global Green Deal would operate in both wealthy and impoverished nations. It would environmentally retrofit human civilization, bringing green technologies to everything from farms and factories to schools and households. The Global Green Deal proposes to kick-start the environmental revolution through a combination of government leadership and market incentives, "to do," as Hertsgaard writes, "for environmental technologies like solar power and green cars what industry and government have already done so well for the computer technologies: launch their commercial take-off."

One of the ultimate goals of Global Green Deal is the kind of democratic, regional, sustainable production of household items under way in Berea. But alas, that happy dream of true balance, in which by rights of social justice I ought to be able to afford furniture made within a day's drive of my home, is not yet fully realized. The prices were quite deservedly high and outside my range. The other beautiful objects for sale, tempting as they were, were things I simply didn't need. Inured to temptation by many years of living in a house too small to accommodate a lot of stuff, I got away with a few small gifts for friends.

Berea's downtown is still pedestrian-friendly, but the town has not been able to entirely combat the usual American sprawl. Motels and fast food huts are farther out, along the interstate, where they are, in truth, convenient for visitors like me. That's where I stayed, walking across my motel parking lot three nights in a row to carry back a Wendy's broccoli potato for dinner, and I was grateful for it.

I was invited to Berea by Carl Kilbourne, a retired Berea College professor of industrial arts and a kindly gentleman of the old school, whom I'd met at an academic conference. He opened doors for me in Berea quite literally. Carl took me to visit the demonstration farm and woodlot of the Sustainable Mountain Agriculture Center, Inc., a non-profit organization started by father-and-son team Bill and Michael Best. They are developing an heirloom seed bank and experimenting with alternative sources of income for small farmers, notably three large greenhouses for tomatoes. I watched while they moved their new portable mill into the woods and cut some of the many necessary stakes from trees felled earlier. Carl also introduced me to Hugh Hendricks, who custom-sawed waste and reject logs (walnut, cherry, curly maple, white oak, and some white pine) for local furniture makers. Hugh's tobacco barn housed stacks of foot-wide lumber on which we sat to wait out a rain squall and discuss philosophy.

Through Carl, I met Berea College forester John Perry. John is a tall, distinguished, forty-ish man, with blue eyes and a native Kentucky drawl. As the eighth college forester, he takes seriously his role as heir to Silas Mason. Mason, hired in 1897, had studied forestry in Europe and was a well-regarded colleague of Gifford Pinchot, Bernard Fernow, and Carl Schenck, the leading foresters in America at the time. Drawing on the European practice of municipal forest ownership for firewood and timber proceeds, Mason soon inaugurated a program to greatly expand the college's negligible land holdings. His stated purpose was to provide fuel and income for the college and land for instruction in forestry.

Tramping around the countryside looking for tracts to purchase, Mason found a series of large springs located at considerable elevation about the town. By 1905, water was flowing by force of gravity five miles to Berea.

Today Owsley Lake at 151 acres is the largest of four lakes that supply the college with water. The college owns the shorelines and surrounding lands and sells excess water to the town and several local water districts. "There's an eagle or two here in the winter, also loons and many waterbirds," John said as we prowled through his demonstration pine and walnut plantings along Owsley Lake. "A quasi-governmental body, the Red Lick Water District, manages the water use." Some of the water money goes back into his budget as utility income, but he wanted to do a full cost accounting to see how things really stood.

"The college does some timber sales but doesn't get much income," he said. "The vast majority of the forest was abused, burned, and eroded farmland. College students worked as forest firefighters in the first half of the twentieth century, but then liability grew too great." Using college archives, John had written a history of Berea College forestry, illustrated by photos of steep, plowed slopes and stands of charred trunks. In the 1960s, the college had its own sawmill, "but it prompted too much cutting," John said, "up to eight hundred thousand board feet a year, which gives you rotation lengths that don't allow for old growth." In the decade he had been college forester, John averaged around 150,000 board feet a year, mostly driven by salvage cutting of pines because of blowdowns from ice storms and tornadoes.

"At one time, the forest did supply wood for college crafts, but there was a lot of waste, so administrators went to buying lumber instead. But I think that as the price of high-grade lumber continues to rise, we may go back to taking our supply from the forest. We still have walnut left. Eventually, construction materials for renovations of college buildings, which occur at about one building per year, should come from our forest." John had considered the trade-offs among various construction materials in light of increasing pressure from some environmental organizations to use wood substitutes like structural steel, concrete, and plastics. "In terms of fossil fuel and everything else that goes into manufacturing it," he concluded, "wood is the most environmentally benign raw material we have."

John hadn't been able to do as much inventorying and planning as he'd hoped because of a lack of equipment and help. He had received a computer only two months earlier, and though he had some student assistants, it was hard to get anything done out in the forest on the usual two-hour shift. Support for his initiatives depended on administrative attitudes, which were variable. He hadn't even been able to update the last forest plan, which was done in the 1950s, but he figured he was harvesting well below mortality rates and would be safe for a while.

Mason wrote the first management plan in 1907. Fuelwood, timber, and water were the major management goals, but so was recreation. Recreational use of the college forest became institutionalized in 1875, when Berea students celebrated the first annual Mountain Day festival with log sawing and ax throwing. What happened in Berea reflects what happened through the twentieth century across the country: a steady increase in the valuation of forests for recreation. Nearly two thousand acres of college forest are now managed solely for recreational use, and timber sales on other acreage have been modified in response to concerns of people who use the forest for social, educational, and spiritual purposes. Activities occur throughout the year and include nature study, picnics, outdoor dramas, rock climbing, jogging, day camps, arts and crafts programs, and archaeology on prehistoric and Civil War sites. Rustic camping can be arranged at a couple of old log cabins. Fourteen miles of hiking trails offer many scenic views, including some old-growth oaks up Davis Hollow, the only such remnant John knew of.

The trail through the stand was well maintained and obviously well used. It was morning, and sunlight on dewy understory leaves gleamed and glistened. Some trees had tags grown into them from early research; noted forester E. H. Frothingham had studied here. Ginseng used to be abundant but had mostly disappeared. John thought it was probably poached, but he was also noticing more and more deer, which love ginseng. The one amenity the college had traditionally not offered was hunting, but John was beginning to consider a doe-only season. It was one recreational impact he thought he might put to good use.

It's hot on a late July afternoon when my husband, Ralph, and I arrive at Falling Creek summer camp for boys near Tuxedo, North Carolina. We're staying in a wooden cabin with screening all the way around instead of windows. The wooden door closes with a rope pull weighted by a rock and slams dependably every time it's opened. The floor is made of planks between which I can see the ground. This is the counselors' cabin, luxuriously appointed with an old armchair and lamp in addition to four bunk beds and a bathroom. Surrounding us are thirty-two more cabins of eight bunks each, housing some two hundred eight- to sixteen-year-old boys. Through the screen beside my upper berth, I can see a red-eyed vireo pause to sing while working through the hemlocks, but I can't hear a thing. A roar of young male voices fills the air—loud voices of bravado, low voices talking confidentially, daring voices, taunting, commanding, encouraging, whistling, yelling, shouting.

*I am not a fat butt! Am not!*

It's rest hour before dinner at Falling Creek, a fully accredited camp of a thousand acres in North Carolina's Blue Ridge. There is surely no more hallowed tradition of childhood than summer camp, and no more honorable way for parents to cope with school vacation. For many children, summer camp is the quintessential experience of nature, one that shapes a lifetime of attitudes and actions. Camps are the most concentrated of recreational impacts, psychological as well as environmental.

*You'll have to go home if you keep this up!*

Few areas of America are as dense with summer camps as western North Carolina. Falling Creek is one of fifty-two camps in the four counties of Jackson, Transylvania, Henderson, and Buncombe. But because it was owned by the pale-but-sunburned president of the Sierra Club, it was the one I visited to examine issues of sustainable recreation.

Chuck McGrady was born in Baltimore because both parents were in medical school there, but he grew up in Florida. After going to law school, he opened his own practice in Atlanta. He joined the Sierra Club. And he joined the Republican Party.

"Georgia hadn't had a Republican governor in a century," he told me on the deck of the dining hall, "so all the bad environmental stuff for the last hundred years was done by Democrats. It seemed natural enough for me to take the other side, especially in opposing boondoggle public works. It's fairly agonizing, because most Republicans can't imagine that a real Republican would be a Sierra Club leader. I say that protecting the environment is a conservative value; we need to go back to our roots. With environmental people, I remind them that Republicans may have forgotten that protecting the environment is like being fiscally conservative—there have been a fair number of significant environmental protection efforts led by Republicans. It seems obvious to me that the environment ought to be, as it originally was, a bipartisan issue."

Chuck joined the Sierra Club mainly to go on outings, for which the club is famous. Established in 1892 as a network of friends of John Muir, the original California tree hugger, the Sierra Club has grown into one of the most effective grassroots-based environmental organizations in America, with a membership of seven hundred thousand.

"As a Sierra Club leader," Chuck said, "I'm very pragmatic. I don't like rhetoric and have fought overstatements. Environmentalists have a way of painting everything black and white, but most things are pretty gray. I don't lack the will to strike out in unconventional directions."

We struck out on a very conventional stroll around camp before dinner. Chuck bought the five-hundred-acre core of the camp in 1989, and over the next couple years, he closed his law practice and moved to a house near Falling Creek. He adds to his land piecemeal as tracts come up for sale. He has political ambitions, but they are deeply affected by his environmental advocacy, especially his efforts to bring septic tank regulations to homeowners along the Green River, which flows through his camp. "It was as nasty a political issue as you could get," he said. Recently he ran in the Republican primary for county commissioner. "Everyone told me I didn't have a chance because of the Sierra Club connection," he reported in his customary wry tone, "but I lost by less than a hundred votes."

Most of the camp infrastructure—cabins, other buildings, parking areas, stables, open playfields, and a lake, linked by paths and a few roads—is situated on about 150 acres. For three months, this part of the camp is used intensively—that is to say, it swarms with boys during every daylight hour. There are so many boys that even the deer are intimidated and stay away. Gangs of boys were leaping off a diving tower in the lake to land on the Blob, an inflated balloon, where they bounced.

*Yaaaaaay! Whoooeeeeeee!*

*Awesome jump, dude!*

At the end of August, the tumult ceases. From September through May, only three staff members live at the camp. "Within a week after the last kids leave," Chuck said, as our path passed through a grove of oaks and white pines, "pileated woodpeckers are hammering here." Beyond the camp basin, Falling Creek encompasses mostly steep, forested slopes and narrow ridges, and a few flat fields along the Green River where the horses are pastured. "We can't make our own hay," Chuck explained, "because it comes due for cutting just when our first batch of boys arrives in June, and we can't handle it all."

During the summer onslaught, there are several waves of impact. Economically, the camps in the four-county area spend more than $50 million on operating expenses and capital improvements every year, much of which goes directly to the local economy. Parents bringing, picking up, and visiting their kids brings in another $20 million.

Environmentally, all those energetic young feet and digestive systems have to be accommodated, and quickly. Septic drainage for most of the cabins runs under the athletic fields away from the spring-fed lake. Newer buildings have their own septic systems. Falling Creek had been established as a camp for twenty years before Chuck bought it, developed from what had been a family summering estate in pre-air-conditioning days, when whole households moved up from Charleston to escape heat, mosquitoes, and malaria.

"Some of the original trails went straight up," Chuck said, "and we've had to reroute them. The roads are also a mishmash. Erosion is a major issue. When I bought the place twelve years ago, the cabin area was highly eroded, with water coming down into the lake carrying all kinds of stuff. We put in railroad ties and rain breaks to slow the water, and we still do a lot of mulching. The water off roofs is a concern, too. The new lodge has more impact than I expected; we're trying to divert the water without washing out our road and filling in the lake." Chuck picked up tiny bits of trash as we passed the canoe hut, the infirmary, and the office.

*Camp nurse: Are you having any trouble breathing?*

There had been some broken bones over the years, but the biggest problem, Chuck found, was parents. "When we have a problem kid and have to contact the parents, we can see why. I don't know what parents think, that they don't need to set rules for their kids. Kids want rules; they will test them, push them—that's what kids do. Five years ago, a third of the boys were on Ritalin. Now it's much less."

Chuck's own eleven-year-old son was attending Falling Creek this session, as he usually did, as well as another camp nearby for a later session. Chuck had spent his childhood summers going to camp and had even worked as a counselor at Falling Creek, years before he thought about buying it.

"Many of my values come out of summer camp," he said. "My sense of community, of connectedness—the old John Muir thing, being hitched to everything else in the universe. When you're at camp, you have a lot of time to spend wandering through the creek. There's an intuitive feeling you have toward nature. Most of the values that have led me to be active in environmental work came out of summer camp. It's often true of environmental leaders that they have a strong sense of place, of special places that need to be left as they are. I try to impart a sense of place and community, not just among the campers or the counselors, but the idea that community is larger than just us. There are animal and plant communities, and they have a future just as the boys do."

Chuck was a founder and past president of the local land trust. He was pursuing the idea of conservation easements with several other interested camp owners nearby. He didn't, though, have a formal land-use plan. The state department of forestry had suggested it assess his land and write a management plan, but Chuck felt their management and his would not be the same.

"I don't have any great need to timber it," Chuck said. "It's fairly common for intensive logging to go on around me, and some logging is not utterly inconsistent with camping. I've had some timber taken on a very selective basis. A local sawmill operator a few years back wanted ten big hemlock trees he saw on my land; it was no big issue for me, as long as he didn't tear up the place getting them. Of course, we use firewood for camp-outs. Basically, I need all the trees I can get to make the forest as natural as possible."

By now we had arrived at the environmental education center. Falling Creek offers instruction in swimming, sailing, white watering, mountain biking, rock climbing, backpacking, horseback riding, riflery, track and field, and basketball, but its proudest achievement is the nature study program. Director Joe Duckett had been developing it for eight years into a nonprofit organization that gives presentations year-round to schools, churches, and other groups. One of Joe's main units is "The Forest," in which he conveys concepts of biodiversity and ecosystems. At camp, Joe directs boys in stewardship projects, such as building steps on eroding trails. Noticing a sphagnum moss bog at the side of the lake, he teamed up with a specialist in pitcher plants to seed the rare species. He leads many hikes, sometimes two per day, and emphasizes observation and identification of plants and animals. His kids catch the same snakes and turtles year after year, some of which grow noticeably tame. Joe has a license to house injured raptors, and the nature hut was home to a great horned owl and red-tailed hawk, as well as snakes, lizards, hellbenders, rodents, and rabbits.

Several years ago, a boy brought Joe a green salamander, a federal species of concern because populations are declining. The salamander was on a tree that was cut the next year to make room for a bath house. Green salamanders rarely use trees; mostly they secrete themselves in dry, shaded rock crevices under mature mixed forests. Two hundred yards away from the bath house is a rock slab where you'd expect to find them, and Joe does, now that he knows to look out for them. Another boy found a salamander in the new shower. Chuck reported the incidents to the state nongame biologist. "He was surprised they were here," Chuck said, "and he didn't have any problems with it."

Pink streaks of sunset were reflected in the lake. The darkening forest canopy on the other side was dotted with the white blossoms of sourwood trees. Our tour was nearly finished. As we walked through a parking lot below the dining hall, I noticed a couple of big SUVs with the camp logo.

Chuck seemed slightly embarrassed. "We just stopped offering water skiing," he said. "It was getting too crowded and unpleasant. Now I can get rid of the SUVs. It's kind of a sore point, the president of the Sierra Club owning these gas guzzlers, but they sure are good for pulling boats."

Some of the camp's activities were conducted not on Falling Creek property, but on nearby national forest lands. Less than a quarter of all private forestland owners allow recreational access to people they don't know. And access keeps shrinking as forestland is parcelized among nonrural owners with little exposure to ideas of the commons. At the same time, the demand for access to natural landscapes is steadily increasing, to the point that many national forests are obviously overused. The debate over user fees and other limits to recreation in national forests must eventually address the role of private lands in absorbing what the national forests can't.

We were just in time for dinner. It was fried fish, french fries, and cole slaw, served family style in big bowls and platters on the table. Dessert came individually wrapped.

*That's my Moon Pie! Gimme back!*

There are serious waste issues when you feed hundreds of some-times persnickety kids. The only disposables used were paper plates and plastic forks at the Sunday cookouts for the whole camp. "We'd like to recycle more," Chuck said, "but we can't get vendors to take more than cardboard and aluminum. There's a lot of food waste. We give it to neighbors who have eight or ten hogs. They love us."

After dinner, everyone drifted gradually back to the cabins. The next morning, Ralph and I planned to hike around Falling Creek. I wanted to recapture the forest through a child's eyes—enchanted, full of mystery—as I had experienced it during my own long-ago days at summer camp. I lay in my bunk anticipating the moist, mossy cove forests of Falling Creek, with their glossy-leaved rhododendrons still harboring a few late blooms. We would find the ancient bus with a Coca-Cola ad that had been there as long as Chuck could remember, but about which he knew nothing. We would find Shangri-La, the remains of a house where, Chuck said, "two so-called odd men had lived, by which I guess they were gay." We would find the Octagon under tall pines, and mushrooms of orange, red, yellow, and white, evidence of a kingdom underground.

But in the meantime, I wondered how in the world we would ever get to sleep in the midst of this clamor. Whistles, bells, roars, strains of guitar and song, blaring boom boxes.

*Get off my bed!*

*That's my pillow!*

*Shut uuuuuup!*

The evening deepened until dark thoroughly saturated the basin and you needed a flashlight to walk along the paths. Then the last bell rang. Nearby, a firm older voice shouted above the din: "Lights out, gentlemen! I'm starting the countdown! Five . . . four . . . three . . . two . . . one!" And, as if cut with a knife, the noise fell off.

The silence was deafening.

# ABSENCE MAKES THE HEART GROW PARANOID

INSTEAD OF HAVING CHILDREN, MY HUSBAND AND I BOUGHT LAND. Our first purchase was thirty-five acres of old farm high on a mountain in Randolph County, West Virginia. Farming stopped by about 1960, and we acquired it in 1971. The slope once plowed for corn had maple saplings that didn't yet overtop me. The former potato patch was in early succession sumac. That part of the forest was young, like us, just setting out in life. West Virginia was the venue for my rejection of all things conventional in early adulthood, which to my astonishment now dates thirty years ago. I'm proud to be an aging hippie, weaned on a slogan of "Peace and love, man."

West Virginia was where we planned to go back to the land. Ours was not the kind of farm you are probably thinking of, with gentle pastures and gracious barn and genteel house. West Virginia has those in its valleys, and our hearts lusted after them as we drove around looking at real estate. But we had too little money, even at the bargain prices of those days. For $5,000, we bought a defunct mountain farm, steep-sloped, slab-sided where the cliffs poke out, with one long, narrow ridgetop along which a house and a few small fields had clung. The house was gone, apparently disassembled and reused elsewhere.

We thought we would make a living there out of sheer beauty. At thirty-two hundred feet, with one of the wettest climates in the East, our land is a high enclave of uncommon plants and birds. But more to the point, it has a cold, short gardening season, and there are few ways to earn grocery money. Compromising our dreams like most normal people, we ended up settling in a lower, less remote area, where gardens and jobs came easier. That is how we came to be absentee landowners. Camping on a patch of flat meadow for decade after decade, I keep finding things I've never noticed before, and not only in the landscape.

We visit once or twice a year, sometimes more, sometimes less. At first we worried terribly about being away, and the lurking threat of vandalism kept us from building anything. Most of our worst fears have never materialized. No one has set the place afire. The ATVs haven't torn the ground up too badly—even the slope where we stopped Jesse Hoover's caravan years ago, carrying sacks of apples to bait deer farther up the ridge, has grass growing on it now. There's not as much new trash these days either, just some pop bottles and plastic bags.

Near the little pool formed by the spring and shadowed by the biggest, oldest oaks on the property are piles of refuse. When we bought the place, the detritus of a lost way of life had been strewn everywhere. Rusted buckets, cables, strands of wire. Lots of glass shards, corroded canning jar lids, broken crockery. Syrup bottles and shoe soles. A simple headboard of iron shafts curving from a center button to the four corners. Pieces of green china with gold bands, others with bright red designs. Two halves of a cup, large, white, stamped with flowers. The pieces could be glued together, and there would only be one tiny, V-shaped chip in the rim.

Once I considered it all trash. Rubbish. Garbage. I resented the way it marred, in my eyes, the natural beauty in which it lay. I resented the people who, in my imagination, threw it so heedlessly into that beauty. For years we spent entire afternoons consolidating it into heaps. Gradually, over the years, as I lived in Appalachia and learned about its history, my attitudes changed. When I picked the broken teacup from the dirt, I began to see the women who had sipped from it. I began to understand that what lay scattered in the earth might be there through no volition of its owners. I began to recognize archaeological middens, the remains of lives inextricably entwined with this land. I see the meadow in corn, and the men who plowed it. I look at the bedstead and think of love-making.

Even the car junkyard looks different to me now. It took us twelve years to discover it, so thoroughly hidden were the dozen vehicles in a brier thicket at one end of the pasture. Two decades more, and the briers have utterly vanished, killed by the shade of young trees. The trees have grown enough to create a uniformly closed canopy, not yet nicked by time and circumstance, and admitting so little light that no understory plants survive. Car bodies and parts stick out with stark clarity. It's inconceivable that the rusting reality of the cars could ever have been invisible.

And not only are they ugly, but they've also proven to be an actual liability. So it was with some horror that I heard myself defending them on the occasion of my mother's first visit to the property. A suburbanite from a large metropolitan area, she was outraged at the sight of the junkyard.

"You should have sued the realtor!" she cried. I laughed.

"Hire someone to get these out of here!" she demanded. I shrugged. Maybe the fatalism so often attributed to mountain people has seeped into me. "They sort of belong here," I said. Sometimes when we visit these days, we picnic on the tailgate of a pink 1950s station wagon.

Our view has grown so cluttered with trees that we can no longer see across the Tygart River valley to the opposite hillside, where stones arranged to spell "Conley" mark the graves of a family killed by Indians in 1777. The two or three small fields along our lane have grown up everywhere into trees except on the low saddle along the ridge. There, a thick, green grass grows very dense and higher than my waist. After thirty years, locust trees are the only species to have become well established on the edges of the meadow. They also grow along the lane beside the other old fields. Locusts are prized for their rot resistance and are used in fence poles. Ours did not go unnoticed.

One Friday evening not long ago, we got an anonymous letter in the mail. It was postmarked West Virginia and addressed very formally to our names in full—obviously taken from the county courthouse land tax records. It read:

> Dear Sir:
>
> I am writing two you, two let you no. They are cutting loctas [locust] tree on your land and taking them sell them two Mill Creek for fence post. [Name] is who is doing it. Check with mill at Mill Creek who the check name is end they have took two loads already end.
>
> Thank you
> A friend

First thing next morning, we jumped into our pickup truck with a rifle rack in the rear window, where we keep an umbrella. We drove the two and a half hours to the property and found that the note was right. Seven of the biggest black locust trees were fresh cut and gone, which the mill confirmed meant a loss to us of $300 to $400. It took us the rest of the day and much of the night to decide what to do about it.

Our first impulse was to go to the sheriff, but we quickly dismissed that idea. The law has so often been an instrument of oppression in Appalachia that attitudes toward its representatives are ambivalent, if not hostile. Besides, legalities were unlikely to offer a satisfactory way of interacting with local people. Maybe, we thought, we should go directly to the people. There was a family of the name mentioned in the note along the road in to our property, and we could stop by. But what would we say? What if there was someone living there with the first name that was specified in the letter? It would be like a court, with us as judges. This, too, was unlikely to be satisfactory. We had only an anonymous accusation. Even though we were grateful for the note, which may have been sent by one of the handful of people we have met there over the years, we couldn't help wondering whether it was part of someone else's feud. We definitely didn't want to get caught up in that.

What we did, finally, was put up a gate. When we first bought the property, Ralph set posts and put a cable across the driveway, but the lock was soon shot off. It was our first experience with the commons. We hadn't had any kind of gate in the quarter century since then. But as we drove far up Old Pointe Mountain Road beyond our property, as we always did when we visited, following the sinuous line of ridge past hunting cabins, pastures, and a scrupulously kept graveyard, we noticed other private roads. They were mostly closed with steel cattle gates and locked with a loop of chain. It was an accepted practice. Now we have a standard, locked cattle gate. We hope it will signal a silent thanks to the person who warned us, and a rebuke to those who caused an open road to be gated. Maybe the community itself will censure the culprits. No more locust trees have disappeared—yet.

Over the years, as the locusts sprouted and grew robust, the many huge chestnut stumps in the woods that flank the ridge have moldered into massive pads of red dust. Each time I come, I fall in thrall to these ruins of giants. Most of the trunks were cut and salvaged after the blight killed them all by the 1940s; none of them are lying on the ground except one enormous, twisted bole in a far corner. When we bought the place, it was still standing, a magnificent, hulking presence. Clearly, American chestnut trees grew well here, to five feet and more in diameter. These were the trees whose wood and rich, dependable nuts were a mainstay of rural life for both humans and wildlife. The loss of chestnuts has seriously diminished the carrying capacity of the land. Some scientists call it the worst ecological disaster ever to hit the eastern United States.

After we settled in Virginia, Ralph and I sometimes talked about selling our West Virginia land. It appreciated slightly over the years, but not nearly enough to outweigh our emotional attachment to it. In a sense, the property is the progeny of our youth, and like a child, it deserves a bright future. With no direct descendants to answer to, we are free to consider the best interest of the land. And that, we decided, is chestnuts. Rather than merely mourn at their long, sad funeral, we wanted to contribute to their restoration. For some years, we've been members of The American Chestnut Foundation (TACF), a nonprofit group dedicated to breeding blight-resistant American chestnut trees. When TACF began searching for places to plant seeds from the third-generation of backcrossing American trees with blight-resistant Chinese chestnuts—nuts that were fifteen-sixteenths American chestnut and ready to be tested in real woods rather than a protected plantation—we offered our West Virginia property. Representatives of TACF traveled there, took one look at the stumps, and accepted.

We are tying our donation to a mutually agreeable management plan that outlines about fourteen acres to be planted, some of which will have to be timbered to accommodate the chestnut trees. The plan also identifies features to be permanently protected, like the big trees around the spring, a grape arbor in a grove of old apple and cherry trees where wildlife comes to feast, and large trees along the property borders, which are a sort of historic resource. TACF agreed to offer its program on chestnuts to local communities and schools. We retain lifetime recreational use of the property, so we can continue camping on our spot, and watching.

For protection against unexpected circumstances that might at some future time cause TACF to sell the land, we considered a conservation easement, a legally binding agreement between a property owner and a public body or authorized conservation group. Easements are officially recorded as part of the property deed and conveyed to subsequent owners. They generally limit the number of parcels into which the land can be divided and allow only those activities that maintain its natural character. But each conservation easement is individual, shaped by the characteristics of each property, so unique features and circumstances can be accommodated. So far, it's the only mechanism available for addressing the ultimate requirement for sustainable forestry: stability. Without that, no long-term forest management strategy—the only kind that matters—can be assured of coming to fruition.

Conservation easements have been around for several decades, slowly growing more popular. A few property-rights extremists attack the idea, claiming that it unfairly restricts future generations. This contradicts their own basic premise, which is that owners should have unrestricted latitude in doing what they want with their property. A conservation easement, being entirely voluntary, is the fullest possible expression of individual property rights.

In addition to ethical advantages, conservation easements also have federal and state tax benefits. We quickly learned that our income was too small to gain much tax relief. But that wasn't why we didn't do an easement.

It was the cars.

In West Virginia, as in some other states, there is no state agency authorized to hold conservation easements. Instead of the state, private land trusts, either national or local, may be legally enabled to hold them. Private land trusts cannot mobilize the power of the state behind enforcement of the easement, if some future owner violates the terms. And that is a very real scenario. Land trusts around the country are finding that as easements signed decades ago pass into third and fourth generations of ownerships, they are being ignored by some landowners. Monitoring the easements it holds, through periodic site visits and by tracking land transaction records in the courthouse, is the most critical function of a land trust.

Monitoring requires staff, and enforcement involves legal expenses. Without taxpayer monies to draw on, private land trusts must secure finances for future operations. It's therefore a common practice to require that the donor of a conservation easement also provide an endowment to maintain it. The sum could be as low as a few hundred dollars for property with no liabilities. This is where the cars come in. For us, the required endowment is $5,000. The problem isn't soil pollution, the usual case with junked cars, because the engines and transmissions were gone even before we bought the land. It's the chance of injury. You just never can tell what might happen. Somebody might try to get behind the still-enticing wheel of the sleek, if degenerated, Dodge, say, and fall through the rotting seat. Naturally, there would be a lawsuit.

Fortunately, TACF was not put off by the cars and considered the liability issue to be rather far-fetched. We decided to trust the foundation's stewardship ethic for the long-term future of the property. There remain only the final details concerning supervision of the logging necessary to prepare for planting chestnuts. Bureaucracy moves slowly, even in nongovernmental groups, but finally we're reaching the point of a written contract. One Saturday morning, as Ralph and I were working out some of the last aspects of the donation, I answered the phone.

"I'm calling from Elkins, West Virginia, for my son," a woman said politely. "He wondered if you were interested in selling your property in Randolph County."

"Oh, well, no, I don't think so," I said, surprised, but not very, because over the years there have been a few inquiries like this. I explained that we were working with The American Chestnut Foundation to plant blight-resistant chestnuts there. She wasn't the least interested.

"What if he offered you a thousand dollars an acre?" she said.

I took the phone away from my ear and looked at it, mouth agape. I heard the woman say something about her son wanting to hunt. She asked if we owned any other land around. I put the phone back to my ear and said no, and she said, "Well, thank you," and hung up.

---

This is a tale of two brothers. The elder by a year and a half, Ches (for McChesney) Goodall III is clean-cut in shirts with button-down collars, a self-employed consulting forester with a master's degree from Duke University and a whiff of Old South in his gracious manner. Pen (for Pendleton) Goodall is rough-looking in flannel shirts and jeans, makes his living as a logger, and is inclined toward action instead of academics. Together they form a partnership to explore a new vision of the property rights of absentee ownership.

The land in question is seventeen hundred acres in Highland County, Virginia, but you have to drive into Pocahontas County, West Virginia, to get there. It was purchased in several stages by their father, beginning in 1949. Over more than half a century, two generations of Goodalls have committed themselves to caring for property that contains relics of a once-common ecosystem that retreated to the mountaintops when the last ice age receded, and that harbors species common in Canada but rare in Virginia. A third generation of Goodall boys is now growing up there. This gives a twist to the definition of "absentee landowner" and blurs the line around "outsider."

The property is riven by Laurel Fork, famous for its beavers and its native brook trout, and an eventual tributary to the Potomac River. All of the land lies above thirty-five hundred feet; the highest point is nearly forty-two hundred feet. Most of it falls within the forest type known as mixed mesophytic, characterized by a rich diversity of hardwood tree species. But at these chilly heights, where frost may fall in any month of the year, there is another kind of forest engaged in an epic Appalachian saga being played out before Goodall eyes: native red spruce.

Before timber companies ran a narrow-gauge railroad up Laurel Fork in 1908, much of this high-elevation region was probably covered by red spruce. Red spruce was originally one of West Virginia's principal timber trees, covering an estimated 469,000 acres. It was almost entirely removed, with less than 50,000 acres remaining today. After the trees were cut, in the same pattern that scarred so much other land in the Appalachians, logging slash fueled unnaturally hot and frequent fires that destroyed much of the soil. Tiny pieces of spruce charcoal still molder in the ground. After the land was cleared, it was common practice to run livestock on it.

"This was an old farm when Dad bought it," Ches said. A remnant meadow, with a pond constantly dimpled by rising trout, filled our immediate view as we stood on the porch of the farmhouse. Scattered hawthorn trees, locally called thornapples for their barbs and small, red fruits, had been sculpted by grazing deer into the

flat-bottomed silhouettes of African acacia trees. Our horizon was ser-
rated by dark spires of spruce. They were not, however, red spruce.

"Dad wanted to re-create what local people said was the original
forest," Ches explained, "but when he first bought the place, only the
seeds for Norway spruce were commercially available." Ches's father
had been born in Staunton in Virginia's Shenandoah Valley, an hour's
drive to the east, and began coming to Highland County as a young
man. Eventually he became a medical scientist of international
renown for his discovery of L-dopa and dopamine. "As we moved
around the country for Dad's career, this was our one real home we
always knew was there," Ches said. "We came here every summer."
Today Ches lives in Richmond, Virginia, and brings his four-year-old
son to the property several times a year.

Norway spruce established an immediate forest cover on some of
the old pastures, with no threat of invasion because the seeds are sterile. Ches and Pen took advantage of the availability of red spruce seeds
to plant a stand in 1985. Ches led me through the dark and fragrant
stand. From this, and from relict stands scattered across the mountains,
spruce saplings are now moving out to reclaim some of their ancient
range. Their spiky branches made dense and prickly thickets in places.

This is the first good news about red spruce in many years. Studies across the Appalachians in the 1960s through the 1980s showed
that the growth rate of red spruce trees was slowing down dramatically. In 1986, a survey of West Virginia found that a third of all red
spruces were dead or declining. Acid rain is the primary suspect, and
although the Clean Air Act of 1990 reduced the sulfur emissions from
industry, nitrogen and other contaminants continue to assault forests.
"Maybe the cattle have been off the land long enough now," Ches
speculated, "to allow spruce seedlings to try again. Red spruce are also
migrating into areas occupied by northern hardwoods, especially black
birch and red maple."

In addition to red spruce, there are also bogs and balds on the
Goodall property. All of these uncommon ecosystem features attracted
the interest of The Nature Conservancy, a private nonprofit group

dedicated to preserving biodiversity. The Goodalls sold the conservancy a two-hundred-acre tract with a remnant stand of old growth in order to buy out two siblings who had never bonded with the place but wanted their share of the inheritance. Ches also hopes to interest the other private landowners on Laurel Fork in conservation easements to create a protected corridor along Laurel Fork between two segments of national forest land that lie nearby. There are only half a dozen other large tracts, and about as many small ones.

"Conservation easements weren't well known when Dad died, which is unfortunate, because that's just what he would have done," Ches said. Instead, his father's will was so vaguely worded that the Virginia Game Department wrangled a public hunting and fishing easement on more than half of the land. "It's been a nightmare," Ches said. "We've had ATV trails, fires, and absolutely no oversight of permits." He has formally proposed that the game department transfer its easement to The Nature Conservancy, where he is also placing an easement for the rest of the property. So far, there's been no response.

Ches's father was a hunter, and a tongue-in-cheek menu on the wall of the house lists haute cuisine sauces for grouse and wild turkey. He gave written permission to local hunters, a system that Ches wants to reinstate when the easements are finally completed. The easement governing the property as a whole will be based on the forest stewardship plan that Ches composed to manage the property over his and Pen's lifetimes. "Management of the timberlands will vary in intensity from strict conservation to intensive forest management . . . implementing sound conservation practices that preserve soils and water quality," it states.

"Income has always had to be one of our objectives," Ches said, as we hiked out of silent spruces into rustling hardwoods up Hull Ridge, "to pay taxes, insurance, and road and house maintenance. We won't cut red spruce—we all feel a reverence for it—but the plan allows us to harvest hardwoods through selective thinning." Ten management units are mapped out in the plan, with about three hundred acres protected from most forms of harvest. Ches abhors diameter-limit cutting—taking out everything above a certain size—and instead marks individual trees of all sizes. He bases his decisions on the idiosyncrasies of each site. He stopped to regard a recently dead, very large oak that stood beside the trail, just inside a zone designated by the plan as a natural area to be left uncut. "This would make some beautiful boards," he said, a bit wistfully. "But I'm tired of doing forestry the traditional way. As a consulting forester, I'm usually paid by a commission from timber sales, so there's an inherent bias to mark as much cutting as possible."

Recommendations in the plan for the remaining fourteen hundred acres run from light thinnings to small clear-cuts, with a general guideline of retaining two-thirds of the overstory. The use of chemicals is permitted occasionally to kill the poorer hardwoods. Buffer strips of at least two hundred feet will be left on either side of a creek bed. Considerations of scenic beauty and native diversity are written into each recommended action.

"If society really wants to move toward sustainable forestry, a lot of logging practices are going to have to change," Ches said. "There shouldn't be much cutting in spring and early summer, when bark is loose and easily wounded. But the main thing is hauling log lengths rather than whole tree trunks out of the woods. Cutting a tree up into log lengths makes it much easier to snake through without banging into every remaining tree. But many sales are by sealed bid, so I don't have any choice about loggers—the highest bidder gets it. That's where Pen comes in."

The family agreed years ago that no one would live on the property. But Pen always wanted to, so in 1983 he bought an adjoining hundred-acre sheep farm. His little boy was born there. From his home next door, using a small skidder and a truck with a loader, Pen cuts and markets an average of about fifteen acres a year from the family property. He saws up most of the branches and scatters them, so they decay quickly, but sometimes he builds brushpiles for wildlife. He is slow and methodical. He'd better be, because it's dangerous work, and he's alone in the woods.

Red oak is the predominant tree, with substantial amounts of black cherry—two of the most valuable timber species in the Appalachians. To avoid repeatedly taking all of the best trees and leaving the worst to shape the future forest, the practice called high-grading, Pen also takes trees that are badly formed, wounded, or diseased for pulpwood or firewood. The earnings pay him a modest salary, cover the expenses of owning the family property, and fund two kinds of scholarships.

Several years ago, the brothers started an annual contribution of $1,000 to a graduating senior at Highland County High School, chosen in conjunction with the school's guidance counselor. Ches also administrates a $2,500 internship to forestry students at Duke University and has a long list of research he'd like to see started, but the long drive makes it difficult to attract students. He's thinking about shifting to a Virginia university.

Along Hull Ridge, we found several recent cuts of an acre or two each. At one place where the skidder went down thirty feet of slope, Pen had put in six or eight water bars. Tender, green shoots were sprouting from seed he had thrown. Still, Ches looked unhappy. "There's no getting around it," he said. "Timber extraction is ugly, especially right afterward. But I think we can harvest in ways that truly improve all forest values, including ecological health."

In another place along Hull Ridge, where all trees had been cut except a handful of large black cherries over a grassy understory, Ches studied the ground closely for seedlings. They were clustered on one side of the trees, blown by wind. There were also some tiny red oaks. Ches geared much of his tree selection toward opening gaps for their shade-intolerant acorn sprouts. As in Pennsylvania, hay-scented ferns and striped maples were problems; we passed whole hillsides of them. Fires might encourage oak regeneration, and Ches had tried an understory burn, but it was too moist here to burn well.

We hiked down and crossed Laurel Fork, barely, sliding on slick rocks. Rhododendrons, known in Appalachia as laurel, hung over the banks. Springs gurgled out from under spruce roots. Warblers and vireos sang above us. Bluets were blooming all along the creek we followed back to the house, where we met up with Pen. The brothers have agreed that the conservation easement should prohibit logging after they die. They hope to establish an endowment to fund the costs of ownership in the future. Forester and logger leaned on opposite sides of a porch post, their shoulders slouching toward sustainability in a family union of urban and rural, residence and recreation, philosophy and action.

# TIMBER AND
# COAL BARRENS

LIKE OTHER MEN WHO BECAME TIMBER BARONS IN NINETEENTH-century America, Truman Doud Collins, known as T. D., had a strong entrepreneurial drive. He was born in 1831 on a farm in New York to parents who were industrious and pious. They borrowed books around the neighborhood for T. D. to read. He attended the Cortland Academy, where he was especially good at mathematics. As a teenager, he set up a business to earn commissions selling butter and eggs from surrounding farms to New York City markets. From his business acquaintances, he started hearing about the log rafts, 350 feet long and 40 feet wide, floating down the Allegheny River to Pittsburgh.

Forest County in northern Pennsylvania was named for its dense woodlands. The little town of Kane in the adjoining county of McKean now calls itself the Black Cherry Capital of the World, but that came later. The Allegheny Plateau originally sported a deep, dark forest of hemlocks and beeches, interspersed with small, pure stands of enormous white pines. Sugar and red maples, birches, and chestnuts were scattered throughout. Widespread timbering in the nineteenth and early twentieth centuries, followed by browsing by Pennsylvania's famously large deer herd, reversed those forest proportions. Today the plateau is covered by mixed hardwoods interspersed with occasional conifers. The landscape is rolling, with occasional sharp defiles and frequent small marshes. The weather tends toward cold and wet. There are two seasons here, people say—winter and the Fourth of July. For something to look forward to, once or twice a century a tornado mows down five-thousand-acre swaths of forest.

Timber rather than farms attracted pioneers to the plateau in the 1850s (coal mining occurred to the south). T. D. began his career there as a surveyor's assistant, carrying the chain. From crews of woodsmen, he learned of the high prices—$20 a thousand board feet for clear lumber—being paid downstream. He assembled a raft and a crew at Tionesta and floated 150 miles, a four-day trip, to Pittsburgh. He invested in a sawmill and land, then more sawmills, more land, and some of the oil and gas wells that were just being drilled. He developed a chemical wood factory that produced charcoal for the steel industry as well as methyl alcohol and acetic acid for acetone. Others like him were doing the same. When the railroads came in after the Civil War, the lumbering, which had been patchy, coalesced into a vast clear-cut across most of the plateau. Steam-powered equipment sent constant sparks, igniting the slash, and the forest burned over and over.

Like other timber barons looking for business after they exhausted Pennsylvania, T. D. Collins went west. His son, Everill, established the family lumber business in the pine forests of northern California and southern Oregon, and today the headquarters of the Collins Companies is in Portland. But unlike most other lumbermen on the plateau, who sold their plundered lands to the U.S. Forest Service and let the government take care of environmental restoration, T. D. kept his Pennsylvania land. The Allegheny National Forest was established all around the original Collins tracts, and the fire protection the Forest Service provided on its own lands helped them as well.

T. D. Collins put much of his Pennsylvania land in a trust for the Methodist Church. Eventually, in the third generation, this proved to be the anchor that held the family in Pennsylvania. The Collinses were the barons that came back. And they brought with them a philosophy and a method to deal with their own legacy.

Rapacity did not come naturally to the Collins family. T. D. was renowned for his frugality (including, some said, his wage rates). He wore plain clothes and worked in the woods and mills with his men. He saved money by avoiding the roistering places in the nearby town of Warren. Raised in the Presbyterian Church, T. D. wasn't religious as a child, but he came to believe that the Almighty had given him a special talent for accumulating money. Early in his timbering career, he was converted to active Christianity by a backwoods Methodist minister appropriately named Reverend Hicks. Around that time, T. D. had a dream, which one account describes as a vision involving the letters "P.C."

Clearly, the Almighty was giving T. D. a jump start on the concept of political correctness. However, T. D. interpreted his dream as a directive to devote his wealth to philanthropic causes. He responded by supporting missionary schools and orphanages around the globe, and donating substantially to Temple University and other educational institutions. Even more notable, he was generous at home and made sure that the communities around his mills had schools and churches. He often declared to his friends that the more he gave, the more successful he became.

After T. D. died in 1914, Everill continued his father's business and philanthropy on the West Coast. He left the Pennsylvania lands in the hands of a competent caretaker and largely forgot about them.

When Everill's son, Truman W., graduated in 1924 with an MBA from Harvard, he had just completed a course called Lumbering and Forestry. Truman was deeply influenced by the concept of sustained yield. Having grown up near the shores of the Pacific Ocean, he realized that the "cut out and get out" mentality of past lumbering had nowhere else to go. He saw, too, that communities and families would fare much better if jobs remained steady over the long term. He formulated a business view of the forest as principal that shouldn't be touched, while the biological growth rate constituted the interest that could be harvested. He established research plots, and every ten years the growth rate in them was measured. Harvest rates were calculated over the next decade to remove no more than that growth rate, and usually less.

Truman took over the family business after his father, Everill, died in 1940. Before deciding whether to sell the Pennsylvania lands to pay estate taxes, he traveled east with the company's chief forester to look them over. The two men tramped around both the Methodist Church trust lands and the remaining family-owned tracts. They found vigorous second-growth trees that were adding two inches in diameter every decade. What's more, about a third of all the trees were black cherries, which were then selling on the stump for nearly $15 per estimated thousand board feet. With the sure instincts of his grandfather, Truman knew there was a valuable future forest here, and that it was worth paying taxes on the land until the forest matured.

Truman persuaded the Methodist Church authorities to forgo the immediate profits of a one-time sale of their trust lands. He prepared a management plan that called for waiting twenty years and then harvesting the larger trees on a selection, sustained-yield basis. In the meantime, he hired a forest manager, who began once again acquiring land. By 1974, as acreage crept up toward the hundred thousand mark, the company built what was then the largest sawmill in Pennsylvania in Kane, which was roughly central to its timber base. To the ten kilns powered by the mill's steam boiler, which runs on sawdust, the company added a solar kiln. It also added a dimension mill, a secondary process that adds value to low-grade and defective lumber by recutting and gluing boards into a variety of products. And it kept buying land.

By the end of the twentieth century, the company owned 125,000 acres in two hundred separate parcels, large and small. This constitutes a little over a third of the total acreage held by the Collins Companies in three states. As a timber company, with a land base under 300,000 acres and annual lumber sales of some $200 million, Collins is small compared to Willamette and other multinational giants. But in Pennsylvania, Kane Hardwood, as this division of the Collins Companies is called, is one of the largest private landowners in the state. Plus, it employs over one hundred full-time people in its two mills, not counting thirteen crews of loggers, who are hired on a contractual basis.

A significant chunk of the ecology and the economy of the Allegheny Plateau is linked to the business decisions of the Collins Companies. Ever since Truman began implementing a strict policy of sustained-yield harvest, the business has been taking its responsibilities with increasing seriousness. In 1994, Collins became the first commercial timber company in the United States to be certified by the Forest Stewardship Council.

This international, nonprofit accrediting group, based in Oaxaca, Mexico, manages one of the fastest-growing of several schemes proposed for forestry certification over the last decade. More than twenty-five million acres, about 0.3 percent of the world's forests, have been certified so far. The council consists of representatives from the timber industry, environmental groups, indigenous peoples, and other interested parties from more than two dozen countries. Through a series of large, regional committees, the council establishes management criteria for many different types of forests. Criteria are precise, detailed, and voluminous, and articulating them has not been without controversy: Several members of the Appalachian committee have resigned because they felt the guidelines were either too lax or too strict.

Certification requires a third-party audit in three areas: timber resource sustainability, forest ecosystem sustainability, and socioeconomic benefits. Kane received high scores in all three. In addition, the Kane mills attained chain-of-custody certification, which requires that every milled board be identified by origin.

This requires Kane's mill yard to have separate log piles of certified and noncertified wood. By far the largest is Collins-grown timber, which supplies between 80 and 90 percent of the mill's production. These logs are sawed into the certified lumber called CollinsWood. Black cherry is the most valuable; nowhere in the world does it grow as well as on the Allegheny Plateau. Indeed, Kane sells off the very best cherry trees for veneer, because its own mill is not equipped for the peeling process that produces veneer. The Kane mill saws about ten million board feet a year of red maple, ash, beech, birch, sugar maple, red and white oak, poplar, and basswood, in addition to cherry. The company policy is to harvest trees according to what the forest has to offer, rather than what the mill needs to maintain full capacity. Logs are milled in batches, and a computerized inventory system of bar-code labels identifies each pack of boards.

High scores are not all there is to certification under the Forest Stewardship Council. The auditors made various recommendations for improvement, such as better inventory methods using geographical software. They also required the establishment of a preserve system to permanently protect some habitat for the twenty endangered species on company lands. And every five years, Kane is required to recertify.

"When comparing [the higher level of 1999] results with 1994," stated the first recertification report, "a clear conclusion to be reached is that the Kane Hardwood personnel, from senior leadership through to recent hires, have all contributed to the substantial advance of sustainable and exemplary forest management."

"We feel certification is the right thing to do," said Blaine Puller, forest manager for Collins and one of its most senior leaders. He had been with Kane since 1975 and had a thick thatch of white hair. Job tenure at Kane is longer than average in the industry, because employees like working for the Collins family. Several of them mentioned that there were times when the family could have made more money by shutting the mill and selling their logs outright, but didn't do so. In the office reception area, there were photos of former CEO James Quinn accepting the Presidential Award for Sustainable Development from President Bill Clinton and the Millennium Award from Mikhail Gorbachev, president of Green Cross International. He was also pictured on the cover of *Timber Processing* magazine as "Timber Man of the Year."

The employees I interviewed were talking about the company's recent adoption of The Natural Step, a Swedish-based program to integrate sustainable practices into all business operations.

"It's the kind of thing," Blaine said, "that spills over to your personal life, makes you think about how you live."

Blaine and other employees were well acquainted with Terry Collins, T. D.'s great-grandson. Terry had come out from his home in California in the early 1980s to work at Kane. He stayed for fifteen years, built a house, and married a local girl before moving back west. The whole family returns to Kane every summer.

The home that Terry Collins built, now used as a company house for visitors like me, is not what you'd expect from a timber baron: It is a modest house in a modest neighborhood, and the closest home to the noisy mill. Except for a wall each of red oak, black cherry, white ash, and white oak paneling sawn by Kane Hardwood, it's an average American middle-class house. No conspicuous consumption here.

When I left the company house to meet Blaine, the morning was threatening rain, as is usual in May, but the day turned suddenly sunny. Light streamed into the forest edge along the backroads we were driving, a forest edge with a prominent deer browse line. Blaine was explaining the differences between certification by the independent Forest Stewardship Council and the timber industry's own Sustainable Forestry Initiative, known as SFI.

"The difference is that industry writes its own rules," Blaine said. "SFI allows clear-cutting and plantations, while the Forest Stewardship Council generally requires natural forests that are managed according to natural disturbance and regeneration patterns. If the industry requires third-party auditing for SFI, which it's starting to do now, the audit proves the industry is abiding by its own rules. The Forest Stewardship Council sets much stricter rules. We require our loggers to take the SFI training, though, because it's very good."

Kane also requires its loggers to use cable skidding, in which a cable is stretched from a skidder on an established road to a tree at the harvest site. Logs are carried along it, which reduces soil compaction from heavy equipment. Most Kane crews consist of two men. One crew uses horses. They were all enjoying a nice day off today, because the ground was still sodden after recent rains. But it was easy to see where they'd been working. Kane uses the two-step shelterwood system, which critics call a modified clear-cut. It's the modifications that matter.

Our first stop was a sixty-acre mature stand of mixed hardwoods. Or rather, it had been; it was now being harvested in the first of the two steps of a shelterwood cut. Fifty to one hundred trees per acre were left standing, mostly in clumps, usually around spring seeps, den trees, and rock outcrops. Clumping the trees helped buffer their sudden vulnerability to windthrow. Each tree was marked with green or orange paint. Green indicated prime specimens left to produce seedlings for the next forest. These were black cherries, sugar maples, and several other species that need direct sunlight to germinate. The mother trees would be harvested in five to ten more years, after they had established seedlings. The orange-marked trees would remain permanently.

"We leave any species that's hard to regenerate or rare," Blaine said. "Also, den trees, any unusual habitat elements, and stream zones. We leave the slash, too. It looks ugly, but it returns nutrients to the soil and makes a lot of woody debris habitat for small wildlife. And it hinders the deer from browsing on seedlings. The race is on," he declared, looking around, "between tree seedlings, deer, and the interfering vegetation."

By "interfering vegetation," he meant a trio of native plants that, given a disturbance from either natural or human causes, often take over a stand: hay-scented ferns, the small tree called striped maple, and beech root sprouts. These are among the few plants that deer don't like. A century of preferential browsing by a lot of deer has resulted in self-perpetuating open savannas of ferns and shady forest thickets of beeches and striped maples. Acid rain may also be changing the soil chemistry in some way to favor these particular plants.

"After two years, we establish research plots to analyze the regeneration," Blaine continued. "Then, if after five years the seedlings meet standards for adequate regeneration, we'll come back in and harvest the green-marked trees. If not, we'll wait another five years. By then the slash will be mostly rotted down. If interfering plants take over, we'll use herbicides; there's just no other way to beat them. If deer are too thick, we may put up fences. We've had to fence many other stands, because deer are our biggest threat. Those are expensive measures, though, so we'll avoid them if we can. But regeneration is our single greatest priority. It drives all our decisions."

As you might expect, hunters are welcome on Kane lands. The roads that are kept gated the rest of the year, to prevent garbage dumping, firewood cutting, and timber theft, are opened from September through January for them. Walk-in access is open to everyone year-round. Unlike the intensely focused hunting at Marcia Bonta's place a few hours' drive to the south, though, hunting on the plateau hasn't been able to keep up with the deer herd.

The second timber cut we visited was the second step in a shelterwood cut, where five years earlier the first cut had removed most of the trees. It looked very much like the first cut we'd just left, except there were fewer trees remaining. One very nice, straight cherry tree stood nearby, and Blaine walked around it, wondering why it had been left.

"There," he said, pointing up. "There's a dead branch stub about twenty-five feet up. Our foresters that marked the trees left this one to make a den hole in twenty or thirty years."

It would be ninety years at a minimum, Blaine said, before any harvesting was done here again. And therein lies the advantage of intensive cutting methods over selection harvesting: After a shelterwood cut or a clear-cut, the woods go undisturbed for many decades, instead of being entered every decade or two by loggers looking for the next round of selection cuts. If access roads are closed after an intensive cut, human interference is minimized. Animals that are vulnerable to human interference, like cougars, can have a long period of benign neglect.

"Our cherry cutting cycle is about a hundred years," Blaine said, "because cherry only lives about a hundred and fifty years at the longest. Oak rotations are a hundred and twenty years. We harvest altogether about two thousand acres a year, less than two percent of our holdings, so we minimize the landscape-scale impacts. We routinely plan ahead forty to fifty years, and the overall plan looks forward two hundred years."

It was clear that this future forest would be mostly cherry, because far more cherry seedlings were volunteering than any other species. The only substantive criticism that Kane has received from local environmentalists concerns its encouragement of a tree that, according to the earliest survey records, composed only 1 percent of the original forest.

"We don't want a cherry monoculture," Blaine said. "To prevent that, we leave sugar maple and beech and various other species, depending on the site."

We drove through miles and miles of forest before the day was over. There were almost more weight limit signs along the narrow roads than houses, and the occasional cottages seemed to be mostly seasonal camps rather than year-round homes. The hemlock woolly adelgid hadn't yet appeared on the Allegheny Plateau, and patches of hemlock stood dark and mysterious here and there. Blaine pointed out some unusually diverse older stands on the original Collins land, where trees of all ages echoed the former forest structure. He thought they might reflect a lighter harvesting on T. D.'s part a century ago. The thought that things might not be as bad as they seem, that some places can be salvaged and some people are committed to trying, was a comfort to me later, at a place where forest would never grow again, and the only thing being sustained was delusion.

––––––––––––

From Cumberland Gap, eastern Kentucky spreads out in long, wrinkled folds of mountains that give way to the sharply puckered hills of the Cumberland Plateau. Here at the southern end of Pennsylvania's Allegheny Plateau, certain mountains in the immediate view bear witness to the coal beds that underlie the region from here to there. Strip mining peels away wide swatches of earth along the contours of coal seams, leaving a sheer cliff on the upslope, mounds of dirt and uprooted trees on the downslope, and an oddly stepped, almost pyramidal silhouette. But that's merely a little landscaping compared to mountaintop removal.

Afternoon haze thickens the view from Cumberland Gap and blurs the landscape into a soft-edged quilt of greens and browns stretching to a blue horizon. Before it was conquered by King Coal, this country belonged to Daniel Boone, at least in spirit. In 1775, years before he became bewildered at the Red River Gorge, he brilliantly laid out the Wilderness Road through a remarkably convenient set of passages in the Cumberland Mountains. Three hundred thousand Americans traversed his route by 1800, mostly on foot, in the nation's first great westward pulse.

But Boone didn't actually discover the gap. Twenty-five years earlier, Thomas Walker and his party were the first white men to travel through what would later be called Cumberland Gap. Walker reported in his journal that during the trip, they had killed 150 wild turkeys, fifty-three bears, twenty deer, thirteen buffalo, eight elk, four wild geese, and much small game. "We might have killed three times as much, had we wanted it," he wrote.

Note the eight elk mentioned in that lineup. Elk inhabited the pre-European forests of eastern Kentucky, but old accounts indicate that they didn't form herds as large as those that inhabited the open grasslands of the West. Eastern Kentucky lies close to the heart of Appalachian biodiversity, and its forests are thick and tangled. Elk would have grazed the many miles of streamside floodplains in the deeply incised valleys, as well as blowdowns and other small, scattered natural openings. And there would have been the old fields, once slashed and burned by Indians for agriculture, but abandoned after several years to revert to forest and regain nutrients.

Early settlers hunted elk wherever they found them. The hides were too bulky to carry long distances to market but were used at home for harnesses and straps. Elk were hunted to extinction in Kentucky before the Civil War began in 1861. In 1997, a collaboration among two state agencies, a private wildlife foundation, and one of the nations's biggest coal companies initiated the largest program in the United States to bring elk back.

In the winter of 1997-98, two hundred elk from Utah were released on coal-mining land owned by Addington Enterprises Inc. near Hazard in Perry County. The plan called for sixteen hundred more transplants over the next decade, as well as natural increase by Kentucky-born calves. The goal was a herd of some eight thousand animals across fourteen counties on the eastern edge of the state. Some of those counties rank among the poorest in the country.

Administration of the project was undertaken by the Kentucky Department of Fish and Wildlife Resources. The Rocky Mountain Elk Foundation, a highly regarded sportsmen's conservation organization based in Montana, contributed $1 million to transport and study the elk. Researchers to study the elk were supplied by the University of Kentucky's Department of Forestry. Addington provided reclaimed surface mines for elk habitat.

Other eastern and midwestern states have reintroduced small numbers of elk and found that the animals can create a significant tourist attraction. Extrapolating from those experiences, officials in Kentucky project revenues in the tens of millions of dollars from hunters and wildlife watchers who would be enticed to the coalfields by elk. Community surveys conducted by the Kentucky wildlife department in the proposed elk habitat area indicated that people mostly supported the project because of the economic gains it promised. Some residents expressed concern about what animals averaging 450 pounds each could do to crop fields, gardens, and vehicles, but many seemed to like the idea of having elk back.

I heard about the elk project through news stories here and there. Eastern Kentucky has always fascinated me. It contains not only the heart of the forest, but also the soul of Appalachian culture. Here remains the strongest refuge of the old lifeways of kinship networks and multiple skills of self-sufficiency. Some of the greatest Appalachian writers, like Jesse Stuart, Harriette Arnow, and James Still, lived in eastern Kentucky. I decided to be one of the first elk ecotourists there. I was already planning a trip when I got a phone call. So starts my story within the story.

"Would you be interested in writing an article on the elk project in eastern Kentucky?" asked an editor for the elk foundation's magazine. They would pay only for long-distance phone calls, not travel, but no matter, since I was ready to pay my own way anyway. I tried to keep the eagerness out of my voice. Assignments from prestigious magazines are rare if you're not a best-selling author or a former president.

I headed down from Cumberland Gap and north to Hazard, the Perry County seat. It calls itself the Hub of the Coalfields and is roughly central to the designated elk habitat. Choppy little peaks of mountains rose above me. If I craned my neck to look back up a creek hollow as I drove by, I'd see a high wall of uniform light green that contrasted starkly with the variegated shades of adjacent forest in full summer leaf. Kudzu spilled over many a strip-mined terrace, looking very tropical as it swallowed whole trees in big-leafed draperies.

There are plenty of modern malls and shopping centers with big parking lots, and most are located on unnaturally flat benches left by mining. In the countryside, there's no predicting what you might see: old log cabins, plywood shacks, trailers, brick ramblers, big white farmhouses, cinder block remains of early gas stations, and abandoned arched buildings of mysterious purpose. Most dwellings have satellite dishes and flower and vegetable gardens. And everywhere there are footbridges, across the numberless creeks.

Of all the fanciful names that mark places in this region—HiHat, Top Most, Pippa Passes, Quicksand, Thousand Sticks, Dwarf, Rowdy—I love Troublesome Creek the most. For me, it evokes that entwining of romance and tragedy that is the essence of Appalachia. I stood on the banks of Troublesome, next to an enormous elm that hosted a garden of mosses and ferns. On the other side of the tree lay a pile of tires, washing one by one into the stream whenever a storm sent rain pulsing down the hills. Like most creeks around here, Troublesome is turbid and sluggish.

North of Troublesome, I turned at Bethel Camp toward Robinson Forest, choosing hesitantly among many beckoning country lanes. It wasn't easy to get to the Boardinghouse Hollow Interpretive Trail, but it was the nearest place to the elk that could show me what the landscape historically looked like. The trail is named for the loggers' lodging that stood near the trailhead in the early 1900s. In the 1920s, after the best trees had been cut, the timber company donated fifteen thousand acres to the University of Kentucky. Robinson Forest eventually became the university's forestry field research and teaching facility. The second-growth woods retain many of the species that make Appalachia a global center of deciduous diversity. Robinson Forest watersheds are some of the most biologically intact left in the region. The Boardinghouse Hollow Interpretive Trail ("Discovering Biodiversity in Eastern Kentucky") is open for the edification of the public, if the public can find it.

Kentucky always seems to be having a heat wave when I visit, but entering the forest provided instant cool respite. The mile-long trail was originally built as a road by the Civilian Conservation Corps in the 1930s to transport materials for a fire tower up to a little knob. The trail guide said there were fourteen numbered steps, but a few had gone missing. Nonetheless, it was possible to detect the subtle differences among forest communities that the guide described—oak hickory, upland oak, and a cove-ravine stand with beeches, big-leaf magnolias, and pawpaw trees. Moss-covered logs lay around. The understory was an uneven carpet of bloodroot, Indian pipe, jack-in-the-pulpit, black cohosh, hepatica, dame's rocket, cardinal flowers along a rivulet, and a multitude of leaf shapes I couldn't begin to identify. Warblers warbled high in the treetops. A barred owl, startled, lifted silently away as I approached. Along the base of a rock cliff, a copperhead lay curled and sleeping.

The fire tower is listed on the National Historic Register and, being still in use, is in good repair. I climbed up the metal steps into a bracing breeze. Below me, the trees of Robinson Forest billowed blue, green, and black like tufts in a great hooked rug. Beyond dark hills spread an encircling band of flat yellow plains, but they were hardly visible through the haze that rose from the respiration of at least thirty thousand different kinds of living creatures.

On my arrival at Addington Enterprises, I opened the conference room door to find a large table around which sat four men. I wasn't expecting a welcoming committee. At least I'd had the sense not to wear a T-shirt with some inflammatory environmental logo, just a plain blouse, shorts, and boots. I was prepared for a hike, not a press conference.

But Addington Enterprises, as represented by its land manager, John Tate, was not one to let a public relations opportunity pass. John had blue eyes, slightly graying hair, and an enthusiastic way of talking. In short, he was good-looking and charming. He had come to Kentucky two decades ago with an engineering company, married a local schoolteacher, and landed a job with Addington.

"I mine coal for a living," he said, "and I'm proud of it." He intended to convince me of the benefits of mountaintop removal and had assembled a team to help him: a lawyer for the University of Kentucky, the elk foundation's regional representative, the state's wildlife programs manager, and a good friend of John's who just happened to be on the Kentucky Commission for Fish and Wildlife Resources.

"I wrote a paper in college totally against surface mining," Doug Hensley said, "but I've come around a hundred and eighty degrees. Somebody could probably blackmail me if they ever found that paper." My laugh was a little nervous.

We took off from the Addington office near Hazard in a convoy of luxurious sport utility vehicles. The Cyprus Amax Wildlife Management Area, also known as Addington's Star Fire Mine, adjoins Robinson Forest. In fact, Robinson Forest is becoming part of Star Fire Mine, as the University of Kentucky slowly liquidates it in return for coal money. We drove by the same swimming holes I'd seen yesterday, probably with the same local children jumping into them.

Then we turned up Ball Fork Drive and, strapped into our cushioned seats, bounced up a coarsely graveled tract. In less than five minutes, we passed from a cool, moist hardwood forest to a hot, dry prairie. Before us spread thousands of acres of grasses waving in the wind.

We stopped and got out. I turned around and around, trying to get my bearings in an alien landscape. The topography was gently rolling, punctuated with sheer cliffs and piles of boulders. Naked rock buttes and long, bare mesas lined the horizon. Sedimentation ponds lodged in unexpected pockets. John drove us to a viewing platform above one of the larger ponds. A sign boasted of the wildlife. Fish dimpled the water. Barn swallows zoomed over it, Canada geese swam in it, and great blue herons hunted the edges. A killdeer cried somewhere close by. John assured me that other species of waterbirds use the ponds during migrating seasons. The elk were known to use them also on hot days like this, twenty to thirty of them crowding into a pool and splashing playfully like children, but we didn't see any.

We drove on, stopping occasionally but venturing only short distances out of our plush, air-conditioned cabs into the searing desolation. Even on flat terrain, I watched my step. The ground was a rough jumble of crushed rocks and plant tussocks. The Surface Mining Control and Reclamation Act of 1977 sets grading standards for reclaimed sites and generally requires that mined lands be returned to their "approximate original contour." Addington and other coal companies dodge the contour requirement through quasilegal variances from state regulators that allow them to blast away hundreds of feet of mountain, scrape out the coal, and bulldoze the rubble into neighboring valleys. Not only does this level the topography, but it also leaves the ground too compacted to grow trees.

To meet the legal requirements for vegetative cover, coal companies plant several species of shallow-rooted grasses. Two or three nonnative wildflowers, notably Queen Anne's lace and butter-and-eggs, splash a little color across the endless fields. To my amazement, thick colonies of coltsfoot grew in the roughest places, where loose spoil clattered like scree under my boots.

Along the drainage runnels of long, bare ridges, shrubs like autumn olive, multiflora rose, and blackberries, and occasionally some black locust and sycamore trees, had gained a foothold and now formed impenetrable thickets. These were sought out by cow elk for calving. The elk lived mostly in the simplified landscape of short-grass prairie and prickly brushland, using brush and forest edges during the heat of the day, but not penetrating very deeply. Without the grass-lands created by mountaintop removal, it would be impossible to sus-tain such a large herd. This was no restoration, but an introduction of elk to an entirely new ecosystem manufactured by humans.

As we drove along, I asked John, "How many acres is Star Fire Mine?"

"I'd rather not get into specific numbers," he replied. "Let's just say we can put elk on our lands for a long time."

The state wildlife agency, however, did have some specific numbers. Based on Landstat satellite images, it determined that of the 2.6 million acres in the fourteen-county elk area, more than 90 percent is forested, while 6 percent, or 156,000 acres, is grassland on reclaimed surface mines. These estimates were based on the best available data, but no money was allotted for ground-truthing, and I turned up some discrep-ancies. A University of Kentucky computer technician demonstrated that some acreage counted as forested was actually open land lying in the shadows of highwalls during the time of day when the satellite passed overhead. The dark shadows fooled the computer. And accord-ing to the Kentucky Bureau for Surface Mining, Reclamation and Enforcement, approximately a million acres have been permitted for mining in eastern Kentucky since 1982. It proved impossible to tease out the statistics for the amount that has actually been mined and reveg-etated, but the best guess is 50 to 65 percent. That's at least half a mil-lion acres, or nearly four times greater than the official estimate by the elk program. Even if mountaintop removal stopped tomorrow, which it wasn't about to, John was right: There was plenty of elk habitat.

No mining was going on at the moment, because of a federal judge's ruling against valley fills, the part of mountaintop removal in which everything but the coal is pushed into neighboring valleys. Many of the legalities had to do with water quality and whether a stream was year-round or intermittent. Hundreds, perhaps thousands of miles of mountain streams had already been buried. Many people vehemently oppose mountaintop removal and have demonstrated their dislike in numerous rallies and political lobbying efforts. But the pause at Star Fire proved brief, with the judge's ruling overturned by a higher court. The blasting resumed, as did legal wrangles on both state and federal levels. Some activists against mountaintop removal foresee that they might eventually be successful, but by then the coal companies will have flattened all the mountains that have any coal in them.

It was quiet up on the plains, with only the wind whistling through all that grass. I saw a grasshopper, and John talked about the vole populations that were developing. The voles are prey for hawks like a harrier I thought I glimpsed. I did see an indigo bunting and a vesper sparrow, and I heard a field sparrow sing. If the elk continue to thrive, there might even be room for a cougar or two. That would bring the total of detectable life forms here to, oh, somewhere around thirty. One-tenth of a percent of the original ecosystem.

John said, "Where else can you build out of the floodplain? You've seen how narrow our valleys are. There's nowhere else to build." He spoke earnestly and gestured toward the expansive, empty view. "This land has become a very valuable resource. It's useful now, where it wasn't before."

Whether it was useful anymore for growing trees was a question being asked in two experiments. Researchers in the university's forestry department had set up a plot on some of the land reclaimed from Robinson Forest. They were proving that by first preparing the ground through an expensive form of plowing called cross-ripping, done with bulldozers equipped with deep tines, trees could be coaxed into growing, although at slow rates. Trees from wild seeds that blow from surrounding patches of forest tend to die after about ten years, as their roots fail to penetrate the earth.

Our last stop was on a ridge overlooking an irregular series of stony little peaks crowning talus slopes maybe thirty feet high. Trees had been planted up and down the slopes. "We left this ungraded under an 'experimental practices' permit," John said. "Some of the best reclamation is none at all. We're trying to push reforestation, planting the most valuable hardwoods and conifers."

In an eerie microcosm of the original topography, the ungraded spoils mimicked on a miniature scale the shape of the mountains they replaced.

"Looks like approximate original contour to me," I said, glad to have something positive to contribute.

Ash, walnut, oak, black cherry, and white pine saplings stood in the withering sun, but only the white pines seemed to be doing well in the drought that was currently under way. No one is sure how the water table will work in mining spoils three hundred feet thick. One study calculated that the rubble aquifer could store plenty of groundwater that could be pumped to the surface for agricultural and industrial use. But theories were no comfort to the trees struggling here, sad and lonely tokens tossed at the notion of sustainability.

"This could be valuable timber in a few years," John said. "There are so many options here now where there were very few before." I turned around to look at him. He flung his arms out to embrace the view.

"I love this land!" he exclaimed.

A little ditty ran through my head and I was almost inspired to burst into song:

Oh, give me a home
Where the SUVs roam
And the deer and the wapiti play
Where seldom is heard
The biodiversity word
And the trees are all three miles away.
Home, home on the mine . . .

But I kept quiet. Maybe John was disappointed in my response, because a little later, his armor of amiability slipped for just an instant.

"If you don't like mining, don't use my product," he said.

Deregulation of electricity is supposed to give consumers a choice of who generates their power. To my mind, it's the only attractive thing about deregulation.

It was high noon. John apologized for not finding any elk for me, and we drove back down from Star Fire to Chaney's Restaurant and Groceries. John and Doug knew the family that ran it and clearly patronized the place whenever they were in the neighborhood.

"Can I bribe you with a five-dollar lunch?" John asked.

"Sure," I said. The menu offered the usual hamburgers, sandwiches, and french fries, but the staff made their own cole slaw and it was good. There was a large, framed reproduction of an elk painting captioned "Into the Cumberland," which Doug had presented to the restaurant and now hung on a wall. On another wall was a large, framed photograph of an early blast at Star Fire, with rocks spewing into the air. The caption stated, "One million pounds of overburden removed." Overburden meant the forest.

John chatted about the future possibilities of the mined land although he did not mention the enormous power plant he was planning to build there. Instead, he spoke of malls, schools, tennis courts, golf courses, factories, office complexes, who knew what. "I'm excited about this," he said. "Can you work with me on it? Can we find some common ground?"


Another thing John neglected to mention was the lawsuit that had just been filed against Addington by eight Perry County residents. They claimed that the company had damaged their property and was illegally using the county road to haul coal. The plaintiffs were led by Pauline Stacy, who lives half a mile down the road from the mine entrance. Her house is a double-wide, but you can't tell because of the way it's so carefully put together. Inside, silk flowers graced the table.

"The blasting broke off the pins that tie the brick to the cinder block," Pauline said. "The two halves of the double-wide shifted, and we had to reinforce the foundations. Bricks on the house are cracked, and so are the garage floor and the pump house. And every day there were seventy-some trucks going by. When it rained, the mud on the road got real thick. When it was dry, the dust was so bad it looked like a bomb had gone off. My husband has black lung and can hardly breathe, so he couldn't go outside."

Pauline is a small woman with short, gray hair and a kind face. She was raised in Blue Grass Coal Camp near Hazard, where her schooling finished at eighth grade. She married and raised two children. A couple years ago, she decided to get her high school diploma. She aced the exams except for math. So she got algebra and geometry textbooks, studied some more, and passed it too.

During this time, she also became a community agitator. She tried to explain the labyrinthine local coal politics to me, but I was soon lost. "Attorneys around here won't hardly take your case against a coal company," she said. Somewhere along the line, she learned about Kentuckians for the Commonwealth, one of Appalachia's most venerable community activism groups. People there supplied her with a lawyer and with help in organizing her neighbors. "If we didn't have Kentuckians for the Commonwealth, we wouldn't have a chance," Pauline said. "The Sierra Club and another environmental group called Heartwood have also helped us some."

Pauline was the first person in her community to work with outside groups against Addington. "There's people around here who work for Addington, and they were scared. When Star Fire shut down, they blamed me. Somebody threw garbage in my yard at four in the morning. Just recently, people have been throwing plastic bottle bombs made with toilet cleanser and aluminum foil. I call the sheriff, but no one comes."

After several years of intensive effort, Pauline won the road case, and the truck traffic stopped. But the number of plaintiffs in the damages suit against Addington went from eight to five as people dropped out for various reasons. Addington offered to settle out of court, and since she would have had to pay for expert witnesses to appear in a court case, Pauline reluctantly agreed.

She then applied her newly acquired organizing skills toward fighting the power plant being proposed for the Star Fire site. "We need jobs, but not at any cost," she said. "The power plant is supposed to burn the coal left in the spoils and reduce the waste from mining, but we don't know what's going to come out of it—mercury, arsenic, maybe other kinds of pollution. We're all going to breathe and drink whatever it puts out. I got a petition of three hundred local names against it, and John Tate promised us a public meeting, but we never did get one."

Pauline was not surprised when it became clear that the power plant was going to be permitted, but some members of the elk partnership were upset at the sudden appearance of a huge factory in the middle of the elk release site. It's likely the elk will be only minimally bothered, though, unless habitat-devouring ancillary development follows the power plant.

"My husband was born and raised here and would never leave," Pauline said, "and we can't afford to move. We'll have to live with the power plant, just like we've had to live with the mining."

And with the elk, too. "I'm for the elk," she said. "But I don't think the coal company ought to take off the tops of the mountains to justify bringing them in." The truth was, though, that she was beginning to have some doubts about the elk. Two or three of them had lived in her yard for about a month during the past spring. Like many other people in the elk zone, Pauline worried about illness, especially chronic wasting disease, a variant of mad cow disease that elk are known to carry, although no sign of it had been reported in the carefully selected and scrutinized elk.

"I wouldn't eat the meat," she said, "and I don't like to have their droppings in the yard. They were poor looking, like they were starving, and they ate my lawn and my flowers."

Elk like gardens. One of the biggest concerns in any eastern elk reintroduction is agricultural damage. Only 1 percent of the fourteen-county elk zone is in agriculture, mostly hay and tobacco fields. The state proposed to cost-share the repair or establishment of fences to protect haystacks from elk, but it's gardens that may need the help. Many yards throughout the area sport the variegated greens of cabbage, corn, and beans, and not for decoration. Gardens are all that get some families through hard times. Money for an eight- to twelve-foot fence to keep elk out, or even the electric strand that could be used around small areas, is not in the family budget.

In an area where hunger has a long tradition, poaching of elk would hardly be surprising. Poaching has, in fact, plagued most elk reintroductions in the East. Yet the half dozen or so cases that had developed so far in Kentucky were less than anticipated. John had pointed this out as a sign of the highly positive local attitude toward the elk.

Well, in all honesty, there was something I hadn't told John, either. I knew I would be seeing elk with or without him, because I had set up an interview with the university researcher who directed the graduate students doing field studies on the animals. Elk interactions with deer, coyotes, and certain species of snails that carry a fatal parasite called brainworm were being monitored in properly scientific fashion. This meant that some elk were collared and could be located at will.

It was surprisingly difficult to navigate by telemetry signals around the plains, though, because the topography changed so quickly and dramatically that maps couldn't keep pace. Most elk stay fairly close to their release sites, but a few wander. A bull that neighbors nicknamed Bullwinkle trekked 135 miles westward to the Ohio River, where he died from heat stress after being tranquilized. A cow wandered some sixty miles east to Grundy, Virginia. To fulfill its commitment to keep elk within the fourteen designated counties, Kentucky wildlife officers shot her after attempts to dart her failed. Several cows moved forty or fifty miles away to calve, but most then returned. Some elk were even observed at an active mine site, peering over a highwall at the motion below. "Don't jump!" yelled the researcher.

The elk are proving themselves adroit at exploring every ironic twist in the terrain. A group of them pulled up $700 worth of plastic flowers while grazing in a cemetery. One was chased by dogs into a dog kennel. Another fell in love with a domestic cow. The worst incidents involve vehicles. At least half a dozen elk have been killed on roads. Some of the cars suffered substantial damage, but no people had been injured yet. In the fall, the elk would also start contending with hunters with the opening of the first elk season. Many yearling bulls were developing branched antlers and had been heard bugling.

It was even hotter on this trip than with John. Just as the graduate student predicted, we found a small herd of elk lying up to their necks in their own favorite swimming hole. We crept silently up a ridge above it, pulling out binoculars. Four adult females, three young calves, and two yearling bulls, probably an extended family group, dozed in the water. They soon caught sight or scent of us and roused themselves, water sluicing off their heavy shoulders, to amble slowly toward some nearby scrub. In the narrow focus of my binoculars, I finally saw the elk as John wanted me to, with only their massive yet nimble bodies filling the view, and no peripheral vision of long, bare ridges or tortured slopes of cobble. Their coats looked shiny and healthy. They walked with a powerful dignity. We watched them for fifteen mesmerized minutes before they disappeared along a well-trodden path into a hillside of thickets.

Later, when I was fighting to save my story from being totally squelched, I cravenly drew on that experience, milking it for enough emotion to make the rest palatable, even using the cliché "majestic." But in the end, nothing was enough. My editor had responded warmly to the article I submitted, and after three months it was beginning to look like I might get away with my take on the elk restoration that wasn't. Then he called unexpectedly.

"This has never happened here before," he said, "and I'm awfully embarrassed about it. I'm having a little problem getting your piece published. Some of the higher-ups don't want to run it. They don't want to offend Addington, which is a big donor." But he thought we might be able to salvage the story if I would agree to certain conditions. Words like "devastated" would be changed to synonyms like "altered." No quotes from Pauline Stacy, no mention of acreage amounts. And I should add a paragraph that expanded my feelings about the elk, conveyed the excitement of seeing them through those narrow-focus binoculars.

"Sure," I said. Better to reach the magazine's readers with a watered-down version, I figured, than not at all. I composed that final paragraph and faxed it in.

Being the author of the first article to be suppressed by this excellent outdoor magazine (at least in this editor's experience) felt like winning some sort of left-handed prize. Having won very few prizes since fifth grade in Catholic school, when a book review of *Gone with the Wind* netted me a cracked statue of St. Francis of Assisi, I wasn't sure how to cope. A nervous wreck as I waited for phone calls, I ran out frequently to the garden to take nose hits on my lavender. And I searched my soul. Could anyone possibly condone mountaintop removal after reading my article? That was the ultimate ethical criterion; everything else was pap.

On important matters like this, I usually consult my husband. He routinely reads my first drafts. Before I faxed it forever, I asked him to read that final, conciliatory but ultimately unsuccessful paragraph that declared the elk "majestic" and hardly mentioned "tortured slopes of cobble" at all. Ralph went through it twice without comment, then gave a long, low laugh.

"You're bad," he said.

It's the nicest compliment he's ever given me.

# HOME SWEET HABITAT

THERE'S NO COAL WHERE WE LIVE, AND NO TIMBER BARONS HAVE ever owned our hundred-acre tract, as far as I know. Yet signs of a tortured past abound. Roads slashed up Cross Mountain long ago are still eroding. Charred stumps recall searing fires fueled by logging debris and by whole trees cut only for their bark from which tannic acid was leached for making leather. A rusting crane sits on a hilltop, abandoned after it wrenched out all the timber it could reach. Moldering chestnut rails snake up a rocky slope with venerable locust trees on one side, sure testaments to a formerly open area. It was probably a desperate effort to grow corn. A little lower, on the plateau where our house sits, a spiderweb of old fence wires is stuck to the ground by different kinds of barbs. Livestock once grazed here. Someone tried to make a living from this land.

The human legacy of Appalachian history is reflected in our neighbors. At one corner of our property border, a small, triangular boundary of land flares out. The county tax map listed no owner. After a while we realized that a squatter lived there in a dilapidated school bus. A middle-aged man with a long, disheveled beard who intones biblical references like a preacher, he might appear alarming to outsiders. A boar's head nailed to a tree at the turnoff to his compound, its face a mask of dry skin and bristles, could be considered odd, especially the ball cap on the boar's head. The man has never caused any problems, though, and lives quietly. When the county auctioned off the land for nonpayment of taxes, the new owner told the squatter to move. The school bus and the boar's head now inhabit the woods farther down a dirt lane, on land whose ownership seems to be uncertain.

From the landless to the commons is not a great leap. Nonetheless, I was unprepared to jump to an entirely different continent to find the commons one afternoon in late September. I was coasting on my bike down a twisting gravel road that forms one border of my property. Two vehicles were parked on the side, and I heard voices in the woods. I stopped and walked into the forest. There were two young boys, the oldest about eight, and two elderly people.

"Hello," I said, smiling. "What are you doing here?"

The older boy stared at me for a moment before he said, shyly, "Mushrooms." He was fair skinned with very large, light blue eyes, and in his hand he held a five-gallon bucket with a couple of small, brown mushrooms at the bottom. The older couple didn't respond but kept turning over logs and poking around the ground; the woman was bent over and never straightened up. She wore a babushka tied at the back of her neck. She muttered something and a younger woman answered unintelligibly, appearing from deeper in the woods. The old man turned his back and mumbled as he walked away.

"Sir," I said, somewhat sharply, "I don't understand you." This rude behavior was irritating. I frowned as the boy and I eyed each other. Then it struck me.

"They're not speaking English?" I asked the boy.

"No." His laconic answer was typical of Appalachian reticence. I've learned not to expect backwoods people I've just met to tell me their names or much else. Trust is a matter of time and personal encounters.

"So," I prompted, "what are they speaking?"

"Ukrainian," he answered.

In a flash, I understood. Quite a number of Ukrainians and other groups have settled in my county over the last ten years. Most are refugees sponsored by local churches. They have fled from oppression or outright terror. Everything has been left behind, except their view of the world. Where the Ukrainians came from, it is customary for families from villages and towns to drive into the mountains and harvest mushrooms. Who cares whose woods these are? It doesn't matter. The woods are a commons that belongs to everyone. Except that here they belong to me.

"Ah, I understand," I said. "But in this country it's customary to ask landowners for permission. Otherwise they might get mad." It is possible for unknown mushroom hunters to get shot if they wander around on just anyone's property.

"I'm not mad," I assured them. The boy interpreted. What a burden for a child. I said, "You're welcome to the mushrooms on my place."

"Thank you," said the grandmother. Perhaps she understood more English than I thought. The grandfather asked the boy to ask me how many acres I owned. When the boy translated one hundred, the old man raised his eyebrows and whistled. He asked, through the boy, if we hunted.

"Da," the boy translated. Yes. The old man nodded slowly.

I invited them to stop by the house, but I haven't seen them since I pedaled away, saying the one Russian word I knew: *"do svidaniia."* "Good-bye," they called out in return. I wish they would come back and ask permission to hunt. In the last few years, after several mild winters, the already abundant deer herd has exploded. Just this morning, I saw six right next to the house. They hardly stopped their browsing when I stepped outside, and I had to clap hard to scare them away from my flowers. Up to a height of four feet, where growth finally overtops a deer's easy reach, the understory is clipped clean by nibbling teeth. Browse lines mark the forsythia hedge and the forest edge, and we fear for our tree regeneration.

When we bought these hundred acres twenty years ago, my husband began teaching himself to hunt. This is unusual. Most men who hunt—and the overwhelming majority of hunters are men—grew up in rural, often blue-collar homes. They learned to hunt from their fathers or other close relatives, and those experiences create one of the strongest bonds among them. They butcher the deer, their wives cook the meat, and their extended families consume it. Hunting is and always was the high point of the seasonal round of outdoor activities that characterize rural life. Boys skip school to go out with their kin, and their younger siblings list "deer season" along with spring, summer, fall, and winter. But Ralph's father grew up in a city, became an electrical engineer, and never went hunting in his life.

Hunting is not easy. It's not something you can simply go out one day and do, at least successfully. It was years before my husband brought home a deer, although several times he passed up sure shots because he couldn't bring himself to pull the trigger. Eventually he shot a buck on a cold, sunny day with brisk winds that covered whatever sound he made. Dressed in camo and blaze orange, which to deer eyes is not the insanely incongruous combination it appears to me, he was following a deer trail. He would move twenty to thirty feet ahead and then stop for five minutes to look and listen. Near the top of the ridge, he stopped next to a triple-stemmed chestnut oak. A doe ran by less than forty feet away. She never saw him, and he realized she was probably being pursued by a buck. He leaned into the oak trees and got ready. Thirty seconds later, a buck trotted over the ridge, coming right at him. As the deer turned slightly aside, my husband shot. The buck went down immediately and didn't get up.

Ralph paused for reflection. He felt no exaltation, but profound relief that the deer had died so quickly. And, he said, he felt thankful. He put a sprig of green pine branch in the deer's mouth, an ancient gesture of gratitude and celebration we learned from hunter friends in Germany. Like childbirth, hunting is a visceral participation in the cycle of life and death. This morning, after I scared the deer out of my yard, I took out a frozen package of venison to cook for dinner. It tastes to me like a communion with the land. When I die, one way or another my remains will go back to the deer. The forest belongs to everyone, and in the end everyone belongs to the forest.

Owning a chunk of the commons has always weighed heavily on us. Over the past twenty years, we've commissioned three management plans. The first was done by a state forester shortly after we bought the land. He recommended clear-cutting and planting pine in most stands. We didn't know much about forests then, but we knew we didn't want to do that. Still, the plan continues to be useful because of the information it compiled about our woods. Another state forester did the second plan, this time through the Forest Stewardship program. It recommended harvesting all our scarlet oaks because they harbor chestnut blight. That seems pointless, because a million acres of national forest behind us is covered with scarlet oak, so we haven't done that either.

The third plan is due soon from Westvaco, a large pulp and paper company that operates in our neck of the woods. Westvaco has been part of Appalachian history for more than a century. Its past is checkered, although even hard-core environmentalists grudgingly admit that Westvaco has made some attempts at change. Like other timber companies, Westvaco offers private landowners a professional management plan and consulting services, all for free. In return, the landowner agrees to provide Westvaco with "the opportunity to submit an offer for any pulpwood, sawtimber, or other forest products produced on these lands, except where such products are harvested for your own use." There is no requirement to actually hold a sale. The term is ten years. Most of our timber is low-quality, so if we wanted to sell any of it, Westvaco would likely be the only market anyway. Using a gentle, cautious, worst-first approach, it might be possible to harvest small amounts of wood through low-impact methods over a very long time span without further impoverishing the forest. Westvaco's plan will probably be a little more ambitious than that, though, and I doubt we will follow it, either.

In the meantime, we support ourselves in other ways from our forest. Wood keeps us warm in the winter. Deer help feed us. I loop together wreaths from grapevines on Cross Mountain and decorate them with pieces of lichen and moss kicked up by the deer. Something sacred emanates from everything I see and smell and touch. A sense of the sacred is what I want to sustain in myself, and in my woods. Given the location of my property, sustainability and sacredness seem to me to take the form of a cougar. I've never seen sign of one here, but sooner or later, with a million acres of national forest at my back door, cougars ought to live in these woods. Whatever my husband and I do with our land must support its future role as cougar habitat in the restoration of the great Appalachian forest. As I walk, I peer at whiskery arrangements of twigs in the shadowy undergrowth, while my back awaits the sensation of cat eyes upon it.

# NOTES

**CHAPTER 1**

**Pages 1 to 11**

"It appears globally, prefixed not just . . ." Sustainable landfills, development, and other activities are defined by Porteous.

"The problem is that the concept . . ." One of the first definitions of sustainable development was made in 1987 by the World Commission on Environment and Development in what is informally called the Brundtland Report to the United Nations: "it meets the needs of the present without compromising the ability of future generations to meet their own needs." While this is an incisive philosophical statement, it is too general to have much on-the-ground applicability.

"Nearly half the world's land was . . ." An extensive body of statistics exists on U.S. and world forests and the global wood products economy, but definitions and measurements vary, and discrepancies appear among the various sets of figures. In such cases, I have tried to stay on the conservative side. Statistics used here are from the Food and Agriculture Organization of the United Nations' *State of the World's Forests, 1999;* the World Resources Institute's *Forests and Land Cover Data Tables;* Brooks's *U.S. Forests in a Global Context;* Powell et al.'s *Forest Resources of the United States, 1992;* Jenkins and Smith's *Business of Sustainable Forestry;* Haynes et al.'s *1993 RPA Timber Assessment Update;* and Birch's *Private Forest-land Owners of the U.S.* and *Private Forest-land Owners of the Southern U.S.*

"It's a quirk of industrial civilization . . ." Southern Appalachian Man and the Biosphere, vol. 4, pp. 1–34; Porteous discusses values in terms of cost-benefit analyses, p. 133.

"Arguments centered on a small, shy . . ." Marchak, p. 59.

"Half of all known plant and . . ." Jenkins and Smith, vol. 1, p. 216.

"So sought after have American hardwoods . . ." Jenkins and Smith, vol. 2, pp. 2–36.

## CHAPTER 2
### Pages 12 to 39

"William brought his Cherokee wife and . . ." There are slight differences between Todd Lester's family history and Bowman; I have used details from both.

"But William Lester was in the . . . " Based on Dunaway's exhaustive research.

"In the 1980s, a coalition of . . ." Drawn from an analysis of the landowner-ship survey titled "Who Owns Appalachia?"

"In the two decades following the . . ." See discussion of poverty and employment on pp. 17–35 in vol. 4 of Southern Appalachian Man and the Biosphere's *Southern Appalachian Assessment Report.*

"Many mountain stories tell of cougars . . ." A large body of cougar folklore, its relation to cougar biology, and the phenomenon of eastern cougar sightings are explored in my book *Mountain Lion: An Unnatural History of Pumas and People.*

"By systematically calculating angles between toes . . ." Dr. Lee Fitzhugh, Department of Wildlife, Fish and Conservation Biology, University of California at Davis, and Dr. David Maehr of the University of Kentucky (formerly the Florida panther program field leader) confirmed photos of Todd Lester's plaster casts of tracks.

"Not that mountain life was any . . ." Salstrom documents declines in antebellum per capita production due to soil depletion and population growth beyond carrying capacity.

"It started with timber. Many families . . ." Eller and Lewis analyze the history of industrialization and logging in West Virginia.

"So it's not surprising that timber . . ." My interpretation is drawn from Waller's compellingly researched book.

"They felled huge oaks, ashes, walnuts . . ." Sizes of trees and the eventual removal of so many walnut trees that hardly a nut was left for squirrels are detailed in Bowman. A 1939 photo of the 582-year-old, 146-foot-high, nearly 10-foot-diameter Mingo Oak is displayed at the Matewan Visitors Center. The picture frame is made from the tree's wood.

"But no public lands were purchased . . ." On illegal means by which coal companies acquired privately held land, see Corbin; also Giardina's moving novel, *Storming Heaven*.

"African-American laborers from the Deep . . ." For a description of the 1907 peonage conviction of the W. M. Ritter Lumber Company of Maben, West Virginia, one of the largest of the timber companies, see Bowman, p. 244.

"Like other miners, he had to . . ." See Corbin and especially Savage for documentation of the Matewan Massacre.

"An early homesteader named the creek . . ." From information available at the Matewan Development Center, Matewan, West Virginia, and from the Matewan website: www.matewan.com.

"They were called "rednecks." They commandeered . . ." Neither Huber's etymological article nor Boney's definition in *Encyclopedia of Southern Culture* mentions the mine wars as a source for the word *redneck*. However, West Virginia resident Joe Aliff links the word with family history on Blair Mountain at the American Folklife Center website, "Tending the Commons: Folklife and Landscape in Southern West Virginia," memory.loc.gov/ammem/cmnshtml/.

"In fact, with coal providing half . . ." Freme, p. 2.

"In places where the virgin timber . . ." Bowman, p. 247, notes Crouch's sawmill of 1933–42 using second growth.

"Read any historical treatment of southern . . ." I am indebted to Kathryn Newfont of the Southern Oral History Program at the University of North Carolina at Chapel Hill for discussions on the Appalachian commons and the difficulties of its historical documentation. See also the American Folklife Center's "Tending the Commons: Folklife and Landscape in Southern West Virginia," memory.loc.gov/ammem/-cmnshtml/.

"The idea of the commons is . . ." In addition to Hardin, I have drawn on Baden and Noonan, Goldman, Anderson, Kay, Fritsch, and the prospectus for "Constituting the Commons," the 8th Conference of the International Association for the Study of Common Property, Bloomington, Indiana, 2000, www.indiana.edu/~iascp/.

"Even today, about two-thirds of the . . ." Brooks, p. 7.

"In addition to Todd's track, verified . . ." Field confirmations of cougars in the East may be found in Bolgiano et al. and at Todd Lester's Eastern Cougar Foundation website, www.easterncougar.com.

"By implication, these cougars aren't entitled . . ." Pyle presents a provocative thesis that closely related taxa may be used to "resurrect" extinct species.

"Inevitably, some have been released or . . ." Personal communication from Roy McBride at the 6th Mountain Lion Workshop, San Antonio, December 2000.

"Now there's even a DNA study . . ." See Culver.

"This is definitely good cougar habitat . . ." See Taverna et al. for an analysis of cougar habitat in central Appalachia.

"I knew he'd been busy setting . . ." The Eastern Cougar Foundation (www.easterncougar.com) is based in North Spring, WV 24869.

"No ecosystem can be biologically (or . . .)" Soule and Terborgh, pp. 39–58, review the role of top carnivores in maintaining biodiversity.

"In the grandest sense, sustainability means . . ." See Grumbine, Irland, and Keddy and Drummond for discussion of top carnivores as essential measures of ecosystem sustainability.

"In the southern Appalachians, a cougar . . ." I am indebted to Susan Morse, carnivore expert and director of Keeping Track of Huntington, Vermont, for discussions on cougar home range in the southern Appalachians.

"A coalition of community, state, and . . ." From material published by the Hatfield-McCoy Recreational Development Coalition, Inc., of Nitro, West Virginia. See also the official website for the Hatfield McCoy Recreation Area, www.trailsheaven.com/.

## CHAPTER 3

**Pages 40 to 61**

"Every year, across the United States . . ." Snyder and Hoffman, p. 295.

"Consulting foresters, as these last are . . ." Baughman, p. 34.

"Their professional organization, the Association of . . ." The Association of Consulting Foresters (www.acf-foresters.com/index.cfm) and the larger, more general organization, the Society of American Foresters (www.safnet.org/), which was founded by Gifford Pinchot in 1900 and has an Appalachian division (www.apsaf.org/), are the oldest but no longer the only major professional organizations for foresters. The Forest Stewards Guild (www.foreststewardsguild.org), based in Santa Fe, New Mexico, and the National Network of Forest Practitioners (www.nnfp.org/), based in Boston, promote ecologically responsible forestry on landscape scales through exploration of alternatives to conventional extractive practices.

"The website for Britt's business, Foresters . . ." Foresters, Inc. (www.foresters-inc.com/index.html), is based in Blacksburg, Virginia.

"It's a common measure in the . . ." For conversion of cubic meters to board feet and a prediction that cubic meters may eventually replace board feet, see Powell et al., p. 123.

"He felt that if the goal . . ." For definitions of ecosystem management as I use it here, see Christensen et al., Grumbine, Irland, Keddy and Drummond, and Yaffee.

"It's getting even harder as forests . . ." Birch and Drummond (1994b), p. 3; Sampson and DeCoster, p. 4.

"That's why acid rain, which leaches . . ." Adams, p. 23.

"Some areas in the Appalachians have . . ." Personal communication from James Roderick Webb, research scientist in the Department of Environmental Sciences at the University of Virginia, concerning his work on streams in Shenandoah National Park, 2000.

"Various associations or guilds of birds . . ." O'Connell et al., p. 1706.

"No protocol exists to monitor soil . . ." Knoepp et al., p. 358; Burger and Kelting, p. 19.

"Christianity has, in fact, been blamed . . ." White, p. 1204.

"Whether the use of BMPs should . . ." Flick et al. review the evolution of regulatory takings theory; Johnson et al. found that fear of regulation has not spurred early harvests by landowners in the Pacific Northwest.

"Gifford Pinchot, whose name Dick had . . ." As quoted in Ellefson et al., p. 421.

"That hasn't happened, although some federal . . ." Flick et al., p. 21, and Baughman, pp. 82–93.

"Water bars and dips are recommended . . ." Swift and Burns give an overview of the impact of roads and BMPs in the southern Appalachians.

"Most southern states have opposed the . . ." Many grassroots, nonprofit organizations across southern Appalachia are working toward mandatory BMPs and stricter state logging regulations as part of a general movement toward sustainable forestry. These include various state Forest Watch groups, which often compile data on sedimentation and other problems from noncompliance; Kentuckians for the Commonwealth (London, Kentucky, www.kftc.org), which is also exploring nontimber uses of woodlots; the West Virginia Highlands Conservancy (Charleston, West Virginia, (www.wvhighlands.org); and Save Our Cumberland Mountains (Lake City, Tennessee, www.socm.org/), which also advocates permits for chip mills based on local timber analyses.

"An audit by the Virginia Department . . ." Virginia Department of Forestry, p. 1.

"Forestry regulations challenge a particular idea . . ." Cubbage (1995) documents the nonabsolute but rather usufructuary nature of property rights.

"Restructuring of capital gains and estate . . ." See McEvoy for analysis of existing legal and financial issues for forest owners.

"Visual beauty, Dick knew, is no . . ." Moore, pp. 14–22, exposes the deficiencies of visual aesthetics as a guide to forest management.

"Money tends to corrupt local economies . . ." McNeely and Sochaczewski give contemporary examples of moving from barter to money.

"This is typical; most nonindustrial private . . ." Baughman, p. 282; Birch (1994b), p. 4.

"More and more small equipment is . . ." Wilhoit and Rummer, p. 3; Sennblad, pp. 11–27.

"But Woodmizer is American. This is . . ." World headquarters of Woodmizer is in Indianapolis (www.woodmizer.com/).

"One of many innovative forestry ventures . . ." Appalachian Sustainable Development (Abingdon, Virginia, (www.mtnforum.org/resources/-library/asd99a.htm), Flaccavento, p. 19. In addition, Appalachian Voices (Boone, North Carolina, www.appvoices.org) has one of the broadest agendas, from fighting air pollution and mountaintop removal to developing informational outreach programs for private forest owners. The Mountain Association for Community Economic Development, known as MACED (Berea, Kentucky, www.maced.org/), is developing a forest resource model with productivity, demand, and change detection modules for twenty-three counties in eastern Kentucky. Appalachia—Science in the Public Interest (Livingston, Kentucky, www.kih.net/aspi) concentrates on nontimber products, waste reduction, and small-scale technology. The Nature Conservancy inaugurated a Forest Bank program in Virginia's Clinch River valley (with headquarters in Abingdon, Virginia) to protect water quality in that global hot spot of aquatic biodiversity. The bank is designed to accept voluntary "deposits" of timbering rights from landowners in return for annual dividends funded by the bank's timber harvesting using sustainable methods (Dedrick et al., p. 22). For efforts by the Western North Carolina Alliance to form a forestry cooperative, see note below.

"Landowners who use foresters for a . . ." Maybe it's a little like letting the fox guard the henhouse to cite forestry research that documents the advantages of hiring a forester, but see Jones.

"One hundred acres is sometimes given . . ." Birch (1994a), p. 4.

"Harry wanted to introduce an entirely . . ." The Western North Carolina
  Alliance (WNCA, Asheville, North Carolina, main.nc.us/wnca/) also
  began to investigate the possibility of establishing a for-profit forestry
  cooperative with the help of the Southern Appalachian Center for
  Cooperative Ownership, Inc. (also in Asheville). WNCA hoped to
  ease the loss of logging jobs caused by decreased timbering on national
  forests by creating jobs for loggers, sawyers, and truck drivers on small
  tracts of private forests using site-specific, environmentally friendly timber management. Washburn in Baughman, pp. 63-68, proposed a
  cross-boundary management organization that was not a cooperative
  but addressed many of the same ecosystem, if not economic, goals, but
  it was never funded (Washburn, personal communication, 2001).

"We are not talking here about . . ." Associations of private forest owners
  exist in every state independently and as affiliates of the National
  Woodland Owners Association, www.nationalwoodlands.org/.

"Cooperatives are economic enterprises that are . . ." Adams and Hansen, p. 23.

"By their very nature, cooperatives cooperate . . ." Data from the International Co-operative Alliance (www.coop.org/ica/index.html), and
  "Cooperatives," *Microsoft Encarta 96 Encyclopedia*.

"Two-thirds of European forests are . . ." Hufnagl, p. 3. Another interesting
  proclamation from the "European Day of Family Forestry" stated that
  forest owners should be compensated for damage caused by air pollution. According to Alexander von Elverfeldt, a German representative
  at the European Day of Family Forestry, forest owners in Germany are
  already largely reimbursed for the costs of liming by helicopters (personal communication, 2000).

"The National Grange, a cooperative for . . ." Personal communication from
  Richard Weiss of National Grange (www.nationalgrange.org/-
  index.html), 2001.

"In less than a decade, a . . ." An overview of forestry cooperatives is available from the University of Wisconsin's Center for Cooperatives
  (Madison, www.wisc.edu/uwcc/) and the Community Forestry Resource Center (Institute for Agriculture and Trade Policy, Minneapo-
  lis, www.forestrycenter.org/). Since forestry co-ops are new, some
  issues remain to be resolved. For example, in an unpublished speech
  made October 22, 1993, at the Forest Policy Center Symposium on
  Ecosystem Management at the Yale School of Forestry and Environmental Studies, William R. Smith of Crowell and Moring Law Firm
  outlined possible antitrust violations if co-ops were deemed to be fix-
  ing the price of timber.

"The ambitious Sustainable Woods Cooperative, based . . ." Sustainable Woods Cooperative (Lone Rock, Wisconsin, www.sustainable-woods.com/).

"The stakes are high: By controlling . . ." Personal communication from Jim Birkemeier, forester for Sustainable Woods Cooperative, November 2000.

"The jargon defines various nuances of . . ." Smith et al. examine every aspect of thinning, pp. 47–129.

"Harry used a four-wheel-drive tractor . . ." Shaffer (1998) gives an overview of tractor logging for farmers; Wilhoit and Rummer review various small-scale mechanized systems.

## CHAPTER 4
### Pages 62 to 91

"In addition, there may be landowner . . ." The Web is dynamic and won't always give the same information from one day to the next. The most permanent sources for information on horse logging are likely to be Jason Rutledge's Healing Harvest Forest Foundation (8014 Bear Ridge Road, Copper Hill, VA 24079, 540-651-6355), *Rural Heritage* magazine (281 Dean Ridge Lane, Gainesboro, TN 38562, 931-268-0655, www.ruralheritage.com), and the North American Horse and Mule Loggers Association (8307 Salmon River Hwy., Otis, OR 97368, 541-994-9765, www.pacinfo.com/~dfrench/horselogging/main.html).

"Most of the two to ten . . ." Cheater; Toms et al., pp. 5–6.

"In British Columbia, where 94 percent . . ." The support for horse logging in the Quesnel District of British Columbia as part of a policy initiative to establish community forestry was described to me in August 2000 by David Zirnhelt, Sr., minister of forests from 1996 to 2000. See also Pynn for a description of the remarkable situation in British Columbia.

"The people who are buying those . . ." Birch (1994a), p. 5. In addition to being better educated, the people who have purchased forestland in the South since 1978 are younger and earn more money than previous forest owners.

"Repeated over a century and more . . ." Nyland, p. 35.

"This was not unusual; many studies . . ." Hicks, p. 191.

"There's fifty million board feet of . . ." For a comprehensive summary of hemlock issues, see McManus et al.

"Examples are red maple, hickory, black . . ." Tift and Fajvan describe the capacity of red maple, a relatively low-value timber tree that has become a special subject of forestry concern, to become dominant in eastern forests.

"The regeneration of oaks in particular . . ." McGee, p. 10, Keyser et al., p. 218.

"The abundance of oaks, and the . . ." Delcourt and Delcourt, p. 342. However, the Delcourts' interpretation of widespread Native American burning is being challenged. Mitchell et al., for example, determined that the Shenandoah Valley of Virginia, which since at least the mid-1800s was said to have been a vast, Indian-burned prairie when European settlers arrived, contained only small openings caused by natural processes and occasional Indian old fields. See also Harmon (1982), Nodvin and Waldrop, Smith and Sutherland, Strosnider, Van Lear and Waldrop, Vose et al., and many of the papers in Stringer and Loftis for the role of fire in southern Appalachia.

"Such fires, as well as other . . ." Davis, p. 166.

"He had visited the Menominee Tribal . . ." Nesper and Pecore describe the Menominee system; see also the Menominee home page at www.menominee.edu/mte/MTEHOME.HTML.

"Even conventional foresters have acknowledged that . . ." Loewenstein et al., Iffrig et al. See also Pioneer Forest home page at www.pioneerforest.com/PF_Home.html. Miller is more cautious about single-tree selection but endorses canopy openings of one-half acre and larger to perpetuate shade-intolerant tree species.

"Studies have found that mechanized skidders . . ." Ficklin et al., Wang. Also, Kalisz and Powell found that minor disturbances such as partial cutting allow native soil macrofauna to persist or reestablish quickly compared with greatly altered soil fauna in fragmented and heavily disturbed forests.

"After years of research, Jason had . . ." Plans for the logging arch are available for $25 but are free with membership in the Healing Harvest Forest Foundation or the North American Horse and Mule Loggers Association (see note above). See Berry (1996) on arch developer Charlie Fisher.

"A survey in Alabama of about . . ." The Extension Forestry Service at Auburn University, Alabama, is a leader in researching the possibilities of horse logging; see Toms et al. for the survey mentioned in the text, and Toms for an extensive discussion of its implications. See Egan for another survey over a twelve-state area from Maine to Ohio that identified significant support for horse logging.

"The American Pulpwood Association (now known ) . . ." Shaffer (1999).

"In Alabama, the survey conducted by . . ." Personal communication from Mark Dubois of the School of Forestry, Auburn University, 2000.

"The median hourly wage of a . . ." Bureau of Labor Statistics, *Occupational Outlook Handbook,* 2000–01 (stats.bls.gov/oco/ocos178.htm#earnings).

"Turman offered a bar-code service . . ." Walker Mountain Sawmill in Bland, Virginia (www.swva.net/turman/m3.html), owned by Turman Lumber Company, charged no premium for Jason Rutledge's horse-logged Draftwood, but was limited in marketing it due to the lack of a kiln. Jim Belcher, sawmill manager, explained in March 2001: "Small custom furniture makers with their own small kilns can use Draftwood, but once we send the boards to a commercial kiln, it's impossible to keep Draftwood separate from other wood. We may be ahead of the curve a little, just trying to get people interested in sustainable forest management." See also explanation of Draftwood at www.draftwood-forestproducts.com.

"The phrase 'nontimber forest products' entered . . ." Chamberlain et al., p. 14. The harvesting of wild mushrooms on national forests in the Pacific Northwest by unemployed loggers and new immigrants in the early 1990s also drew attention to nonforest timber products; competition for mushrooms may have led to one or more murders.

"Faculty there began investigating how nontimber . . ." Hammett and Chamberlain, p. 144, state that the nontimber forest products sector may be growing more rapidly than the timber industry. See also the Virginia Tech Special Forest Products website at www.sfp.forprod.vt.edu/.

"The diversity of the Appalachian forest . . ." See Bailey for an analysis of nonforest products harvested in West Virginia.

"And scientists have indeed found that . . ." Robbers and Tyler, p. 237.

"Ginseng has been one of the . . ." Carlson, p. 238, gives an average of 381,000 pounds of ginseng exported annually from the United States from 1821 to 1899.

"Beneath the canopy lies one of . . ." Ruchhoft, p. 2.

"This family, like so many others . . ." Harriette Arnow's novel, *The Dollmaker,* deserves far greater recognition than it receives today for its depiction of the Appalachian migration to industrial centers.

"Wild roots have been shown to . . ." Robbins, p. 20. Also, Laura L. Murphy, a researcher at Southern Illinois University's School of Medicine, stated in a letter dated June 19, 2001, that Syl Yunker's wild-grown roots were "approximately four times more potent than our standard [ginseng extract] in inhibiting human prostate cancer cell growth."

"Ginseng likes calcium. 'The plants reflect . . .'" Some growers advocate soil amendments of calcium sulfate (instead of lime, which is calcium carbonate) to promote ginseng growth while still keeping soil acid enough to discourage fungi, but the efficacy of this is controversial, and as a method of growing, it is contrary to Syl Yunker's standards for virtually wild ginseng. For an analysis of the calcium issue, see "Producing and Marketing Wild Simulated Ginseng in Forest and Agroforestry Systems."

"An analysis of the American ginseng . . ." Robbins, pp. 69, 79. See also Fredericksen for a comparative analysis of the impacts of logging and development in central Appalachia.

"He later posted these photos and . . ." Syl Yunker used the Herb Growing and Marketing Network at herbworld.com/.

"Ginseng exports more than tripled through . . ." Robbins, pp. 26, 29, and Shipley.

"Some families still dig ginseng, often . . ." Hufford (1997a), p. 13.

"Ginseng poaching is known to be . . ." Personal communication from Andy Hankins, Virginia Cooperative Extension Service, 1999.

"Academic researchers are investigating the genetic . . ." Rebecca Anderson, doctoral student under Dr. Sabine Loew at Illinois State University, cites a necessary population size of 170 ginseng plants at www.bio.-ilstu.edu/loew/ginseng.htm.

"Several such organizations sponsored workshops where . . ." The Appalachian Ginseng Foundation, established by director Al Fritsch of Appalachia—Science in the Public Interest, Mount Vernon, Kentucky (www.kih.net/aspi) not only sponsors ginseng-growing workshops, but also provides dozens of scholarships to enhance attendance by small woodlot owners. The Appalachian Regional Commission, a federal-state alliance established by Congress in 1965 for economic development of a thirteen-state region along the Appalachian Mountains (www.arc.gov/), supports workshops and other activities of a program called Wild Harvest Sector through partnerships with Total Action Against Poverty (based in Roanoke, Virginia, www.taproanoke.org/), Virginia Polytechnic Institute, Craig County Rural Partnership, and West Virginia Cooperative Extension. The Center for Economic Options in Charleston, West Virginia (www.centerforecon-options.org/), promotes sustainable forestry-related microbusinesses such as ginseng growing. The Rural Action Sustainable Forestry Program in Trimble, Ohio (www.ruralaction.org/forestry.html), teamed up with the National Center for the Preservation of Medicinal Herbs

(Meigs County, Ohio, www.ncpmh.org/) and United Plant Savers (East Barre, Vermont, plantsavers.org/) to produce conferences on growing and conserving Appalachian herbs.

"During the 1990s, nearly nine thousand . . ." *American Ginseng,* p. 1.

"Shenandoah National Park successfully prosecuted a . . ." E-mail communication from Lyn Rothgeb, Shenandoah National Park, August 13, 1998.

"It's said that some of the . . ." High, p. 49.

## CHAPTER 5

### Pages 92 to 125

"The principle of 'sustained yield' became . . ." Steen, p. 6. Aplet et al., p. 157, analyze fallacies in the traditional concept of sustained yield in light of new understanding of dynamic ecological processes.

"Pennsylvania's troubles with overabundant deer herds . . ." Redding gives a history of deer populations and forest cutting in parts of Pennsylvania.

"A disharmonic convergence of time and . . ." McShea et al., pp. 24, 271, 303. See also Halls for a biological overview of deer and Nelson for cultural as well as biological issues of deer abundance.

"Growing wood as an agricultural crop . . ." Jenkins and Smith, vol. 1, p. 235.

"Trees that have been genetically engineered . . ." Brown briefly summarizes genetic modifications of trees under way in the United States and the potentially catastrophic problems they can cause to wild forests.

"It's difficult to determine the amount . . ." Salim and Ullsten, p. 93.

"Carbon dioxide is the gas that . . ." The report of the Intergovernmental Panel on Climate Change (www.ipcc.ch/), issued in January 2001 as an international scientific consensus, projected a rise in the earth's average surface temperature by 2.5 to 10.4 degrees Fahrenheit by 2100 due to carbon emissions. Buzby and Perry describe a computer simulation of the impact of higher temperatures on stream ecology in the central Appalachians.

"Studies began to find that the . . ." Harmon (2001), p. 29; Schulze et al., p. 2059.

"More than half of all commercial . . ." Powell et al., p. 9.

"A hundred and fifty new chip . . ." Pressley and Jehl examined the chip mill controversy for the *Washington Post* and *New York Times,* respectively; regional media also cover it extensively. In response to vociferous concerns about chip mills, in 1998 the U.S. Forest Service initiated the Southern Forest Resource Assessment (www.srs.fs.fed.us/sustain/).

Conducted with close cooperation from southern state forestry agencies, the U.S. Fish and Wildlife Service, the Environmental Protection Agency, and the Tennessee Valley Authority, the project compiles and analyzes all levels of forest data available in the Forest Service's thirteen-state Southern Region. The goal of the assessment is to "provide an ecological context that transcends political boundaries." The final report highlighted urbanization and sprawl as major threats to forests, which delighted the timber industry. But the report also documented many other troubling facts, including these: Between 1953 and 1997, the South's timber production more than doubled, its share of U.S. production increased from 41 to 58 percent, and its share of world production increased from 6.3 to 15.8 percent. The American South now produces more timber than any country in the world. Pine plantations increased from about two million acres in 1953 to thirty-two million in 1999, much of which was previously growing hardwood or mixed forests, and pine plantations are predicted to increase to fifty-four million acres by 2040. The southern Appalachians were one of three subregions (with the Piedmont and the lower Atlantic and Gulf Coastal Plains) singled out by the report as areas where the impacts of human population growth and biological threats to forest health may be most dramatic.

"I had seen gullies higher than . . ." I am indebted to Rutherford County soil consultant and Kudzu Kid Caroline Edwards for a tour of her farm and its gullies.

"Willamette Industries began as a lumber . . ." See the Willamette website at www.wii.com/.

"The goal of the Dogwood Alliance . . ." The Dogwood Alliance (www.-dogwoodalliance.org/) is based in Asheville, North Carolina.

"Forced to segregate, college president William . . ." Berea College president William G. Frost is also famous (or infamous) in Appalachian history for having coined the phrase "our contemporary ancestors." Peck, pp. 53, 72.

"Associations of all kinds, from old-fashioned . . ." According to Fred White, chief forester for The Forestland Group of Chapel Hill, North Carolina, timber investment management organizations (TIMOs) owned fourteen million acres by 2001, much of it purchased from timber companies.

"This perspective on the issue of . . ." See Hertsgaard for an analysis of global population trends and links to environmental degradation and social justice.

"A more pragmatic course of action . . ." Global Green Deal (www.global-greendeal.org/) is based in San Francisco.

"I was invited to Berea by . . ." See Kilbourne's analysis of value-added techniques for sustainable regional forestry.

"Falling Creek is one of fifty-two . . ." Falling Creek Camp (www.fallingcreek.com/) is located in Tuxedo, North Carolina. Statistics in this section come from a 1999 economic survey by the Appalachian Regional Development Institute of Appalachian State University.

"Established in 1892 as a network . . ." The Sierra Club (www.sierraclub.org/) is based in San Francisco.

"Several years ago, a boy brought . . ." Corser, p. 120.

"Less than a quarter of all . . ." Southern Appalachian Man and the Biosphere, vol. 4, p. 157.

## CHAPTER 6

### Pages 126 to 139

"For some years, we've been members . . ." The American Chestnut Foundation (chestnut.acf.org/) is based in Bennington, Vermont.

"A legally binding agreement between a . . ." I am indebted to Faye Cooper, conservation easement specialist with the Virginia Outdoors Foundation, and Rodney Bartgis, of The Nature Conservancy's Joint Central Appalachian Program, for discussions on conservation easements. See Diehl and Barrett for an overview of the issues involved.

"Red spruce was originally one of . . ." Strausbaugh and Core, p. 46.

"Studies across the Appalachians in the . . ." Hornbeck and Kochenderfer, p. 199.

## CHAPTER 7

### Pages 140 to 164

"He was born in 1831 on . . ." Biographical information on the Collins family comes from several unpublished works by Terry Collins in Kane Hardwood company files and from Casler. In addition, Jenkins and Smith include a case study of the Collins Companies.

"The Allegheny Plateau originally sported a . . ." Marquis, p. 4.

"In 1994, Collins became the first . . ." Binole, p. 24.

"This international, nonprofit accrediting group, based . . ." The International Standards Organization and the American Forest Foundation Tree Farm Program also offer forms of certification. The U.S. branch of the Forest Stewardship Council (fscus.org/html/index.html) is based in Washington, D.C. It includes Pennsylvania state forests and some other public lands, a smattering of forest industry lands, sawmills and other facilities, and large landowners. See Society of American Foresters, p. 6; Elliott, p. 8; and Butt and Price, p. 3.

"The employees I interviewed were talking . . ." The U.S. branch of The Natural Step (www.naturalstep.org/index.html) is based in San Francisco.

"SFI allows clear-cutting and plantations, while . . ." The Sustainable Forestry Initiative was adopted in 1994 by the American Forest and Paper Association (www.afandpa.org/about/about.html). With more than four hundred commercial timber companies and related organizations as members, the AF&PA represents manufacturers of over 80 percent of the paper, wood, and forest products produced in the United States. Adherence to SFI is a requirement for membership, and AF&PA states that more than a dozen members have been expelled for failure to uphold the SFI standards. Standards for SFI were drafted after surveys were conducted on the timber industry and its image among the general public. A panel of representatives from environmental, academic, and public interests reviews the program periodically. See Kim for a news article on the rivalry between SFI and the Forest Stewardship Council.

"The only substantive criticism that Kane . . ." The Allegheny Defense Project (P.O. Box 245, Clarion, PA 16214, www.alleghenydefense.org) is a nonprofit organization for the protection and restoration of forest communities and diversification of the Allegheny Plateau economy. It is concerned largely with timber sales in the Allegheny National Forest.

"Elk would have grazed the many . . ." I am indebted to David S. Maehr, director of elk field research at the University of Kentucky, for information about historic and current elk ecology.

"As we drove along, I asked . . ." Wunsch et al., pp. 1–2, states that the Star Fire operation will mine seventeen thousand acres in three major watersheds and create five thousand acres of mountaintop removal lands by 2010, but does not give a source for these estimates.

"No mining was going on at . . ." See Ward's extensive coverage of Judge Haden's October 1999 ruling in West Virginia against valley fills.

"Researchers in the university's forestry department . . ." Graves, p. [2].

"No one is sure how the . . ." See Wunsch et al. for an analysis of Star Fire Mine hydrology.

"Somewhere along the line, she learned . . ." Kentuckians for the Commonwealth (www.igc.org/ifps/casestud/gencom/kftc.htm) is based in London, Kentucky.

"The Sierra Club and another environmental . . ." Heartwood (www.heartwood.org/home.htm), an association of groups, individuals, and businesses concerned with native central hardwood forests mostly on public lands, is based in Bloomington, Indiana.

## CHAPTER 8

**Pages 165 to 170**

"It recommended harvesting all our scarlet oaks . . ." Stringer and Loftis, p. 235.

"Westvaco has been part of Appalachian . . ." Westvaco merged with Mead to become MeadWestvaco in January 2002.

# BIBLIOGRAPHY

Adams, Frank T., and Gary B. Hansen. *Putting Democracy to Work: A Practical Guide for Starting and Managing Worker Owned Businesses.* Rev. ed. San Francisco: Berrett-Koehler Publishers, 1992.

Adams, Mary Beth. "Acidic Deposition and Sustainable Forest Management in the Central Appalachians, USA." *Forest Ecology and Management* 122 (1999): 17–28.

American Folklife Center. "Tending the Commons: Folklife and Landscape in Southern West Virginia." Washington, DC: Library of Congress, 1999. memory.loc.gov/ammem/cmnshtml/.

*American Ginseng* (Panax quinquefolius), *Great Smoky Mountains National Park.* Report received from Nancy Gray, Office of Public Affairs, in 1999. N.p., n.d., 8 p.

Anderson, E. N. "Reevaluating the Tragedy of the Commons." *Conservation Biology* 12, no. 6 (December 1998): 1168–72.

Andersson, Kelly. "Horse-Logging." *Rural Heritage* 20, no. 1 (winter 1995): 11–18.

Aplet, Gregory H., et al., eds. *Defining Sustainable Forestry.* Washington, DC: Island Press, 1993.

Appalachian Regional Development Institute. *The Economic Impact of Organized Camping in the Western North Carolina Counties of Buncombe, Jackson, Henderson and Transylvania.* Boone, NC: Appalachian State University, 1999.

Arnow, Harriette. *The Dollmaker.* New York: Avon Books, 1972.

Austin, Richard Cartwright. *Beauty of the Lord: Awakening the Senses.* Atlanta: John Knox Press, 1988.

Baden, John A., and Douglas S. Noonan, eds. *Managing the Commons.* 2nd ed. Bloomington, IN: Indiana University Press, 1998.

Bailey, Brent. "Social and Economic Impacts of Wild Harvested Products." Ph.D. diss., West Virginia University, 1999.

Baughman, Melvin J., ed. *Proceedings: Symposium on Non-industrial Private Forests: Learning from the Past, Prospects for the Future.* St. Paul: Minnesota Extension Service, 1996.

Berry, Wendell. "Trees for My Son and Grandson to Harvest." *Draft Horse Journal* (spring 1996): 40–45.

——. *The Unforeseen Wilderness: Kentucky's Red River Gorge.* San Francisco: North Point Press, 1991.

Binole, Gina. "Mavericks in a Herd Business." *Business Journal* (March 20, 1998): 24.

Birch, Thomas W. *Private Forest-land Owners of the Southern U.S.* Resource Bulletin NE-138. U.S.D.A. Forest Service, Northeastern Forest Experiment Station, 1994a.

——. *Private Forest-land Owners of the U.S.* Resource Bulletin NE-134. U.S.D.A. Forest Service, Northeastern Forest Experiment Station, 1994b.

Birch, Thomas W., et al. *Characterizing Virginia's Private Forest Owners and Their Forest Lands.* Research Paper NE 707. Radnor, PA: U.S.D.A. Forest Service, Northeastern Research Station, 1998.

Bolgiano, Chris. *The Appalachian Forest: A Search for Roots and Renewal.* Mechanicsburg, PA: Stackpole Books, 1998.

—— et al. "Field Evidence of Cougars in Eastern North America." Paper presented at the 6th Mountain Lion Workshop, San Antonio, December 12–14, 2000. Proceedings in publication.

——. *Mountain Lion: An Unnatural History of Pumas and People.* Mechanicsburg, PA: Stackpole Books, 1995.

Boney, F. N. "Rednecks." In *Encyclopedia of Southern Culture,* edited by Charles R. Wilson et al. Chapel Hill: University of North Carolina, 1989.

Bonta, Marcia. *Escape to the Mountain.* South Brunswick: A. S. Barnes, 1980.

——. *Appalachian Autumn.* Pittsburgh: University of Pittsburgh Press, 1994.

Bowman, Mary Keller. *Reference Book of Wyoming County History.* Parsons, WV: McClain Printing Co., 1965.

Brendler, Thomas, and Henry Carey. "Community Forestry, Defined." *Journal of Forestry* 96, no. 3 (March 1998): 21–23.

Brooks, David J. *U.S. Forests in a Global Context.* General Technical Report RM-228. Fort Collins, CO: U.S.D.A. Forest Service, Rocky Mountain Forest and Range Experiment Station, 1993.

Brown, Joshua. "Losing the Forest for the (Genetically Engineered) Trees." *Wild Earth* 11, no. 2 (summer 2001): 46–51.

Bureau of Labor Statistics. *Occupational Outlook Handbook.* Washington, DC: U.S. Department of Labor, 2000–01.

Burger, James A., and Daniel L. Kelting. *Soil Quality Monitoring for Assessing Sustainable Forest Management.* Special Publication no. 53. Madison, WI: Soil Science Society of America, 1998.

Butt, Nathalie, and Martin F. Price, eds. *Mountain People, Forests, and Trees: Strategies for Balancing Local Management and Outside Interests; Synthesis of an Electronic Conference of the Mountain Forum, April 12–May 14, 1999.* Harrisonburg, VA: Mountain Institute, 2000.

Buzby, Karen M., and Sue A. Perry. "Modeling the Potential Effects of Climate Change on Leaf Pack Processing in Central Appalachian Streams." *Canadian Journal of Fisheries and Aquatic Sciences* 57, no. 9 (September 2000): 1773–83.

Carlson, Alvar W. "Ginseng: America's Botanical Drug Connection to the Orient." *Economic Botany* 40, no. 2 (1986): 233–49.

Casler, Walter C. *Teddy Collins Empire, a Century of Lumbering in Forest County: Nebraska, Golinza, Kellettville, Mayburg, Bucks Mills, Iron City, Pigeon, Marienville.* Corry, PA: self-published, 1976.

Chamberlain, Jim, et al. "Non-timber Forest Products: The Other Forest Products." *Forest Products Journal* 48, no. 10 (October 1998): 10–20.

Cheater, Mark. "When Loggers Use Horse Sense to Help Protect Forests." *National Wildlife* (April–May 1998): 14–15.

Christensen, Norman L., et al. "The Report of the Ecological Society of America Committee on the Scientific Basis for Ecosystem Management." *Ecological Applications* 6, no. 3 (August 1996): 665–85.

Collins, Terry. *Collins Pennsylvania Forest: A Human History.* N.p., n.d.

Corbin, David Alan. *Life, Work, and Rebellion in the Coal Fields: The Southern West Virginia Miners, 1880–1922.* Urbana: University of Illinois Press, 1981.

Corser, Jeffrey D. "Decline of Disjunct Green Salamander *(Aneides aeneus)* Populations in the Southern Appalachians." *Biological Conservation* 97 (2001): 119–26.

Cubbage, Fred. "Federal Environmental Laws and You." *Forest Farmer* 52, no. 3 (January 1993): 15–18.

Cubbage, Fred, and John Godbee. "Forestry Best Management Practices Are in Your Future." *Forest Farmer* 53, no. 1 (January-February 1994): 15–17, 24.

Cubbage, Frederick W. "Regulation of Private Forest Practices." *Journal of Forestry* 93, no. 6 (June 1995): 14–20.

Culver, Melanie. "Molecular Genetic Variation, Population Structure, and Natural History of Free-Ranging Pumas *(Puma concolor)*." Ph.D. diss., University of Maryland, 1999.

Davis, Mary Byrd, ed. *Eastern Old-Growth Forests: Prospects for Rediscovery and Recovery.* Washington, DC: Island Press, 1996.

Dedrick, Jason P., et al. "The Forest Bank, an Experiment in Managing Fragmented Forests." *Journal of Forestry* 98, no. 3 (March 2000): 22–25.

Delcourt, Paul A., and Hazel R. Delcourt. "The Influence of Prehistoric Human-Set Fires on Oak-Chestnut Forests in the Southern Appalachians." *Castanea* 63, no. 3 (September 1998): 337–45.

Diehl, Janet, and Thomas S. Barrett. *The Conservation Easement Handbook.* San Francisco: Trust for Public Land, 1988.

Dunaway, Wilma. *The First American Frontier: Transition to Capitalism in Southern Appalachia, 1700–1860.* Chapel Hill: University of North Carolina Press, 1996.

Egan, Andy. "Clashing Values at the Urban Fringe: Is There a Niche for Horse Logging?" *Northern Logger and Timber Processor* 47, no. 1 (July 1998): 16–19.

Ellefson, Paul, et al. "State Forest Practice Regulatory Programs: An Approach to Implementing Ecosystem Management on Private Forest Lands in the United States." *Environmental Management* 21, no. 3 (1997): 421–32.

Eller, Ronald D. *Miners, Millhands, and Mountaineers: Industrialization of the Appalachian South, 1880–1930.* Knoxville: University of Tennessee Press, 1982.

Elliott, Chris. *World Wildlife Fund Guide to Forest Certification.* Godalming, England: World Wildlife Fund-UK, 1997.

Elliott, Katherine J., et al. "Vegetation Dynamics after a Prescribed Fire in the Southern Appalachians." *Forest Ecology and Management* 114 (1999): 199–213.

Ficklin, Robert L., et al. *Residual Tree Damage during Selection Cuts Using Two Skidding Systems in the Missouri Ozarks.* Piedmont, MO: Missouri Department of Conservation, n.d.

Fitzharris, Tim. *Forests: A Journey into North America's Vanishing Wilderness.* Toronto: Stoddart Publishing Co., 1991.

Flaccavento, Anthony. "Building an Ecobusiness Infrastructure in Appalachia." *In Business* (September–October 1999): 19–21.

Flick, Warren A., et al. "Public Purpose and Private Property." *Journal of Forestry* 93, no. 6 (1995): 21–24.

Food and Agriculture Organization of the United Nations. *State of the World's Forests, 1999.* www.fao.org/forestry/fo/sofo99.

Ford, William M., et al. "Effects of a Community Restoration Fire on Small Mammals and Herpetofauna in the Southern Appalachians." *Forest Ecology and Management* 114 (1999): 233–43.

Franklin, Jerry F., and Richard H. Waring. "Distinctive Features of the Northwestern Coniferous Forest: Development, Structure, and Function." In *Ecosystem Analysis: Proceedings, 40th Annual Biological Colloquium, 1979, Corvallis, OR.* Corvallis: Oregon State University Press, 1980.

Fredericksen, Todd S. "Impacts of Logging and Development on Central Appalachian Forests." *Natural Areas Journal* 18, no. 2 (1998): 175–78.

Freme, Fred. "U.S. Coal Supply and Demand: 2000 Review." In *Official Energy Statistics from the U.S. Government.* Energy Information Administration. eia.doe.gov/2000.

Fritsch, Al, ed. *The Forest Commons.* Mount Vernon, KY: Appalachia—Science in the Public Interest, 1997.

Giardina, Denise. *Storming Heaven: A Novel.* New York: Ballantine, 1987.

Goldman, Michael, ed. *Privatizing Nature: Political Struggles for the Global Commons.* New Brunswick, NJ: Rutgers University Press, 1998.

Graves, Donald H. *Starfire High Value Tree Reclamation Project: Progress and Continuation Report.* Lexington: University of Kentucky Department of Forestry, 1999.

Greene, John L., and William C. Siegel. *The Status and Impact of State and Local Regulation on Private Timber Supply.* General Technical Report RM-255. Fort Collins, CO: U.S.D.A. Forest Service, Rocky Mountain Forest and Range Experiment Station, 1994.

Grumbine, R. Edward. "What Is Ecosystem Management?" *Conservation Biology* 8, no. 1 (March 1994): 27–38.

Halls, Lowell K. *White-Tailed Deer: Ecology and Management.* Harrisburg, PA: Stackpole Books, 1984.

Hammett, A. L., and J. L. Chamberlain. "Sustainable Use of Non-traditional Forest Products: Alternative Forest-Based Income Opportunities." In *Proceedings, Natural Resources Income Opportunities on Private Lands Conference.* Hagerstown, MD, 1998, 141–47.

Hardin, Garrett. "The Tragedy of the Commons." *Science* 162 (December 13, 1968): 1243–48.

Harmon, Mark. "Fire History of the Westernmost Portion of Great Smoky Mountains National Park." *Bulletin of the Torrey Botanical Club* 109, no. 1 (January–March 1982): 74–79.

Harmon, Mark E. "Carbon Sequestration in Forests." *Journal of Forestry* 99, no. 4 (April 2001): 24–29.

Haynes, Richard W., et al. *The 1993 RPA Timber Assessment Update.* General Technical Report RM-GTR-259. Fort Collins, CO: U.S.D.A. Forest Service, Rocky Mountain Forest and Range Experiment Station, 1995.

Hertsgaard, Mark. *Earth Odyssey: Around the World in Search of Our Environmental Future.* New York: Broadway Books, 1998.

Hicks, Ray R. *Ecology and Management of Central Hardwood Forests.* New York: John Wiley, 1998.

High, Ellesa Clay. *Past Titan Rock: Journeys into an Appalachian Valley.* Lexington: University Press of Kentucky, 1984.

Hornbeck, James W., and James N. Kochenderfer. "Growth Trends and Management Implications for West Virginia Red Spruce Forests." *Northeastern Journal of Applied Forestry* 15, no. 4 (1998): 197–202.

Huber, Patrick. "A Short History of 'Redneck': The Fashioning of a Southern White Masculine Identity." *Southern Cultures* 1, no. 2 (winter 1995): 144–66.

Hufford, Mary. "American Ginseng and the Culture of the Commons." *Orion* (autumn 1997a): 11–14.

———. "American Ginseng and the Idea of the Commons." *Folklife Center News* 19 (winter-spring 1997b): 3–18.

Hufnagl, Natalie, trans. "European Day of Family Forestry, Hanover, August, 2000." Unpublished paper, sponsored by the European Community.

Iffrig, Greg F., et al. "A Case Study for Sustainable Forest Management in the Missouri Ozarks: 45 Years of Single-Tree Selection Harvests and an Economic Model for Income Production." Paper presented at the Environmental Sustainability and Public Policy Conference, University of Missouri, Columbia, March 4–5, 1999.

Irland, Lloyd C. "Getting from Here to There: Implementing Ecosystem Management on the Ground." *Journal of Forestry* 92, no. 8 (1994): 12–17.

Jehl, Douglas. "Logging's Shift South Brings Concern on Oversight." *New York Times,* August 8, 2000.

Jenkins, Michael B., and Emily T. Smith. *The Business of Sustainable Forestry: Strategies for an Industry in Transition.* 2 vols. Washington, DC: Island Press, 1999.

Johnson, Rebecca L., et al. "NIPF Landowners' View of Regulation." *Journal of Forestry* 95, no. 1 (1997): 23–28.

Jones, Stephen B. "Ecosystem Management on NIPFs: A Mandate for Cooperative Education." *Journal of Forestry* 92, no. 8 (August 1994): 14–15.

Kalisz, P. J., and J. E. Powell. "Invertebrate Macrofauna in Soils under Old Growth and Minimally Disturbed Second Growth Forests of the Appalachian Mountains of Kentucky." *American Midland Naturalist* 144, no. 2 (2000): 297–307.

Kay, Charles E. "The Ultimate Tragedy of Commons." *Conservation Biology* 11, no. 6 (December 1997): 1447–48.

Keddy, Paul A., and Chris G. Drummond. "Ecological Properties for the Evaluation, Management and Restoration of Temperate Deciduous Forest Ecosystems." *Ecological Applications* 6, no. 3 (1996): 748–62.

Keyser, Patrick D., et al. "Enhancing Oak Regeneration with Fire in Shelterwood Stands: Preliminary Trials." *Transactions of the 61st North American Wildlife and Natural Resources Conference* (1996): 215–19.

Kilbourne, Carl G. "A New Sustainable Cash Crop for Mountain Farmers." *Appalachian Heritage* 28, no. 2 (spring 2000): 13–18.

Kim, Queena Sook. "Timber Industry Goes to Battle over Rival Seals for 'Green' Wood." *Wall Street Journal,* May 23, 2001.

Kline, Jeffrey D., et al. "Fostering the Production of Nontimber Services among Forest Owners with Heterogeneous Objectives." *Forest Science* 46, no. 2 (May 2000): 302–11.

Knoepp, Jennifer D., et al. "Biological Indices of Soil Quality: An Ecosystem Case Study of Their Use." *Forest Ecology and Management* 138 (2000): 357–68.

"Land and Life in the Mountains: The Findings, in Brief." *Southern Exposure* 10, no. 1 (January-February 1982): 40–48.

Lewis, Ronald L. *Transforming the Appalachian Countryside: Railroads, Deforestation, and Social Change in West Virginia, 1880–1920.* Chapel Hill: University of North Carolina Press, 1998.

Loewenstein, E. F., et al. "Changes in a Missouri Ozark Oak-Hickory Forest during Forty Years of Uneven-Aged Management." In *Proceedings, 10th Central Hardwood Forest Conference,* edited by K. S. Gottschalk and S. L. C. Fosbroke, 159–64. General Technical Report NE-197. U.S.D.A. Forest Service, 1995.

Mannon, Anita G. "Horselogging: An Alternative to Fuel-Driven Skidders." *Pennsylvania Forests* (winter 1997): 16–18.

Marchak, M. Patricia. *Logging the Globe.* Montreal: McGill-Queen's University Press, 1995.

Marquis, David A. *The Allegheny Hardwood Forests of Pennsylvania*. General Technical Report NE-15. Broomall, PA: U.S.D.A. Forest Service, Northeastern Forest Experiment Station, 1975.

McEvoy, Thom J. *Legal Aspects of Owning and Managing Woodlands*. Covelo, CA: Island Press, 1998.

McGee, Charles E. "Loss of *Quercus* spp. Dominance in an Undisturbed Old-Growth Forest." *Journal of the Elisha Mitchell Scientific Society* 102, no. 1 (1986): 10–15.

McManus, Katherine A., et al., eds. *Proceedings: Symposium on Sustainable Management of Hemlock Ecosystems in Eastern North America, Durham, NH, 1999*. General Technical Report NE-267. Newtown Square, PA: U.S.D.A. Forest Service, Northeastern Research Station, 2000.

McNeely, Jeffrey A., and Paul S. Sochaczewski. *Soul of the Tiger: Searching for Nature's Answers in Exotic Southeast Asia*. New York: Doubleday, 1988.

McShea, William J., et al., eds. *The Science of Overabundance: Deer Ecology and Population Management*. Washington, DC: Smithsonian Institution Press, 1997.

Miller, Gary W. "Maintaining Species Diversity in the Central Appalachians." *Journal of Forestry* (July 1998): 28–33.

Mitchell, Robert D., et al. European Settlement and Land-Cover Change: The Shenandoah Valley of Virginia During the 18th Century. Grant report. National Geographic Society, 1993.

Moore, Patrick. *Green Spirit: Trees Are the Answer*. Vancouver, BC, Canada: Greenspirit Enterprises Ltd., 2000.

Nelson, Richard. *Heart and Blood: Living with Deer in America*. New York: Knopf, 1997.

Nesper, Larry, and Marshall Pecore. "The Trees Will Last Forever." *Cultural Survival Quarterly* (spring 1993): 28–31.

Nodvin, Stephen C., and Thomas A. Waldrop, eds. *Fire and the Environment: Ecological and Cultural Perspectives, Proceedings of an International Symposium*. General Technical Report SE-69. Asheville, NC: U.S.D.A. Forest Service, Southeastern Forest Experiment Station, 1991.

Nyland, Ralph D. "Exploitation and Greed in Eastern Forests." *Journal of Forestry* 90, no. 1 (January 1992): 33–37.

O'Connell, Timothy, et al. "Bird Guilds as Indicators of Ecological Condition in the Central Appalachians." *Ecological Applications* 10, no. 6 (2000): 1706–21.

Peck, Elisabeth S. *Berea's First Century, 1855–1955*. Lexington: University of Kentucky Press, 1955.

Porteous, Andrew. *Dictionary of Environmental Science and Technology*. 3rd ed. Chichester, England: John Wiley, 2000.

Powell, Douglas S., et al. *Forest Resources of the United States, 1992*. General Technical Report RM-234. Fort Collins, CO: U.S.D.A. Forest Service, Rocky Mountain Forest and Range Experiment Station, 1993.

Pressley, Sue Anne. "Chipping Away at South's Forests." *Washington Post*, June 3, 2000, A1, A7.

*Producing and Marketing Wild Simulated Ginseng in Forest and Agroforestry Systems.* Virginia Cooperative Extension Publication 354–312. Blacksburg: Virginia Polytechnic Institute, 2000.

Pyle, Robert Michael. "Resurrection Ecology: Bring Back the Xerces Blue!" *Wild Earth* 10, no. 3 (fall 2000): 30–34.

Pynn, Larry. "Logging with Horse Power." *Canadian Geographic* 111, no. 4 (August 1991): 30–35.

Redding, Jim. "History of Deer Population Trends and Forest Cutting on the Allegheny National Forest." *Proceedings, 10th Central Hardwood Forest Conference,* edited by K. S. Gottschalk and S. L. C. Fosbroke, 214–23. General Technical Report NE-197. U.S.D.A. Forest Service, 1995.

Robbers, James E., and Varro E. Tyler. *Tyler's Herbs of Choice: The Therapeutic Use of Phytomedicinals.* New York: Haworth Herbal Press, 1999.

Robbins, Christopher S. *American Ginseng: The Root of North America's Medicinal Herb Trade.* Washington, DC: TRAFFIC North America, 1998.

Ruchhoft, Robert H. *Kentucky's Land of the Arches.* Rev. and enl. ed. Cincinnati: Pucelle Press, 1986.

Salim, Emil, and Ola Ullsten. *Our Forests, Our Future: Report of the World Commission on Forests and Sustainable Development.* Cambridge, England: Cambridge University Press, 1999.

Salstrom, Paul. *Appalachia's Path to Dependency.* Lexington: University Press of Kentucky, 1994.

Sampson, Neil, and Lester DeCoster. "Forest Fragmentation: Implications for Sustainable Private Forests." *Journal of Forestry* 98, no. 3 (March 2000): 4–8.

Savage, Lon. *Thunder in the Mountains.* Elliston, VA: Northcross House, 1986.

Schulze, Ernst-Detief, et al. "Managing Forests after Kyoto." *Science* 289 (September 22, 2000): 2058–59.

Sennblad, Gotthard. *Small Scale Technology in the Forest: Equipment, Technology and Methods.* Translated by Joakim Hermelin. Garpenberg, Sweden: Swedish University of Agricultural Sciences, 1993.

Shaffer, Robert M. *Farm Tractor Logging for Woodlot Owners.* Publication no. 420–090. Blacksburg: Virginia Polytechnic Institute, 1998.

———. *The Myth of Horse Logging.* Technical Release 99-R-6. Rockville, MD: American Pulpwood Association, 1999.

Shipley, Sara. "Ginseng: Biologists, Conservationists Fear for Future of Popular Herb." *Louisville [Kentucky] Courier-Journal,* September 24, 2000.

Smith, Danna, ed. *Forest Management for the 21st Century: Perspectives of Southern Foresters, Loggers, Sawmill Owners and Landowners.* Asheville, NC: Dogwood Alliance, 1999.

Smith, David M., et al. *The Practice of Silviculture: Applied Forest Ecology.* 9th ed. New York: John Wiley, 1997.

Smith, Kevin T., and Elaine K. Sutherland. "Fire-Scar Formation and Compartmentalization in Oak." *Canadian Journal of Forest Research* 29, no. 2 (February 1999): 29–34.

Smith, Nancy Sue. *History of Logan and Mingo Counties, Beginning in 1617.* N.p., n.d.

Snyder, Thomas D., and Charlene M. Hoffman. *Digest of Education Statistics, 1999.* Jessup, MD: U.S. Department of Education, 1999.

Society of American Foresters Task Force on Forest Management Certification. *Report.* 1999.

Soule, Michael E., and John Terborgh, eds. *Continental Conservation: Scientific Foundations of Regional Reserve Networks.* Washington, DC: Island Press, 1999.

Southern Appalachian Man and the Biosphere. *The Southern Appalachian Assessment Report.* 5 vols. Atlanta: U.S. Forest Service, Southern Region, 1996.

Steen, Harold K., ed. *History of Sustained Yield Forestry: A Symposium, Western Forestry Center, Portland, OR, Oct. 18–19, 1983.* Forest History Society, 1984.

Stewart, Dean. "Wildlife and Forest Landowner Cooperatives." *Forest Landowner* (July–August 2000): 29–30.

Strausbaugh, P. D., and Earl L. Core. *Flora of West Virginia.* 2nd ed. Morgantown: West Virginia University, 1970.

Stringer, Jeffrey W., and David L. Loftis, eds. *Twelfth Central Hardwood Forest Conference: Proceedings of a Meeting Held at Lexington, Kentucky, February 28, March 1–2, 1999.* Asheville, NC: U.S.D.A. Southern Research Station, 1999.

Strosnider, Robert K. "The Role of Fire in the Appalachian Hardwoods." In *Wilderness and Natural Areas in the Eastern United States: A Management Challenge,* edited by David L. Kulhavy. Nacogdoches, TX: School of Forestry, Stephen F. Austin State University, 1986.

Swift, Lloyd W., Jr., and Richard G. Burns. "The Three Rs of Roads." *Journal of Forestry* (August 1999): 40–44.

Taverna, Kristin, et al. *Eastern Cougar* (Puma concolor couguar): *A Habitat Suitability Analysis for the Central Appalachians.* Charlottesville, VA: Appalachian Restoration Campaign, 1999.

Tift, Brian D., and Mary Ann Fajvan. "Red Maple Dynamics in Appalachian Hardwood Stands in West Virginia." *Canadian Journal of Forestry Research* 29, no. 2 (February 1999): 157–65.

Toms, Christopher William. "Whoa, Mule: Animal-Powered Logging at the End of the Twentieth Century." Master's thesis, Auburn University, 1999.

Toms, C. W., et al. "Horse and Mule Logging in Alabama: A Small-Scale Harvesting Option for the Future?" In *Proceedings of International Symposium on Integrating Environmental Values into Small Scale Forestry.* International Union of Forest Research Organizations P3.08.00 Small-Scale Forestry Symposium, Vancouver, BC, Canada, 1998. In press.

Van Lear, David H., and Thomas A. Waldrop. *History, Uses, and Effects of Fire in the Appalachians.* General Technical Report SE-54. Asheville, NC: U.S.D.A. Forest Service, Southeastern Forest Experiment Station, 1989.

Virginia Department of Forestry. *BMP Effort, Implementation, and Effectiveness Field Audit,* June 2000.

Vose, James M., et al. "Using Stand Replacement Fires to Restore Southern Appalachian Pine-Hardwood Ecosystems: Effects on Mass, Carbon, and Nutrient Pools." *Forest Ecology and Management* 114 (1999): 215–26.

Waller, Altina L. *Feud: Hatfields, McCoys, and Social Change in Appalachia, 1860–1900.* Chapel Hill: University of North Carolina Press, 1988.

Wang, Lihai. "Assessment of Animal Skidding and Ground Machine Skidding under Mountain Conditions." *Journal of Forest Engineering* (July 1997): 57–64.

Ward, Ken. "What Now for Coal? Dire Predictions May Be Overblown, Records Indicate." *Charleston Gazette,* October 24, 1999.

White, Lynn, Jr. "The Historical Roots of Our Ecologic Crisis." *Science* (March 10, 1967): 1203–7.

"Who Owns Appalachia?" *Southern Exposure* 10, no. 1 (January–February 1982): 33.

Wilhoit, John, and Bob Rummer. "Application of Small-Scale Systems: Evaluation of Alternatives." Paper no. 995056, presented at the ASAE (American Society of Agricultural Engineers)/CSAE-SCGR Annual International Meeting, Toronto, Canada, 1999.

Williams, Ellen M., and Paul V. Ellefson. "Going into Partnership to Manage a Landscape." *Journal of Forestry* 95, no. 5 (1997): 29–33.

Wisdom, Harold W. "The Chip Mill Conflict: A Wake-up Call for a Comprehensive Virginia Forest Policy?" *Virginia Issues and Answers* 7, no. 1 (spring 2000): 10–18.

World Resources Institute. *Forests and Land Cover Data Tables, Sources and Technical Notes, 1998–2000.* Washington, DC: World Resources Institute, 2001. www.wr98_fo_notes/.

Wunsch, David R., et al. *Design, Construction, and Monitoring of the Ground-water Resources of a Large Mine-spoil Area: Star Fire Tract, Eastern Kentucky.* Lexington: University of Kentucky Geological Survey, 1992.

Yaffee, Steven L. "Ecosystem Management in Practice: The Importance of Human Institutions." *Ecological Applications* 6, no. 3 (August 1996): 724–27.

# INDEX